CAFÉ SOCIETY

Café Society

Edited by

*Aksel Tjora and
Graham Scambler*

CAFÉ SOCIETY
Copyright © Aksel Tjora and Graham Scambler, 2013.

All rights reserved.

First published in 2013 by
PALGRAVE MACMILLAN®
in the United States—a division of St. Martin's Press LLC,
175 Fifth Avenue, New York, NY 10010.

Where this book is distributed in the UK, Europe and the rest of the world, this is by Palgrave Macmillan, a division of Macmillan Publishers Limited, registered in England, company number 785998, of Houndmills, Basingstoke, Hampshire RG21 6XS.

Palgrave Macmillan is the global academic imprint of the above companies and has companies and representatives throughout the world.

Palgrave® and Macmillan® are registered trademarks in the United States, the United Kingdom, Europe and other countries.

ISBN: 978–1–137–27592–9

Library of Congress Cataloging-in-Publication Data is available from the Library of Congress.

A catalogue record of the book is available from the British Library.

Design by Newgen Knowledge Works (P) Ltd., Chennai, India.

First edition: November 2013

10 9 8 7 6 5 4 3 2 1

Contents

List of Figures   vii
List of Contributors   ix

Introduction   1
Aksel Tjora and Graham Scambler

1   The Café as a Third Place   7
    Ray Oldenburg

2   Heart of Urbanism. The Café: A Chapter of Cultural History   23
    Bodil Stenseth

3   *The Theory of the Café Central* and the Practice of the Café Peripheral: Aspirational and Abject Infrastructures of Sociability on the European Periphery   43
    Paul Manning

4   Cafés, Third Places, and the Enabling Sector of Civil Society   67
    Graham Scambler

5   The Café Community   87
    Ida Marie Henriksen, Tomas Moe Skjølsvold, and Ingeborg Grønning

6   Communal Awareness in the Urban Café   103
    Aksel Tjora

7   Becoming a Barista   127
    Eric Laurier

8 Community and Social Interaction in the Wireless City: Wi-Fi use in Public and Semi-Public Spaces   147
   Keith N. Hampton and Neeti Gupta

9 Design for Solitude   173
   Erling Dokk Holm

10 The City, the Café, and the Public Realm in Australia   185
    Peter Walters and Alex Broom

Index   207

Figures

3.1	K. Zdanevich's "Old Tbilisi Sketches"	50
3.2	"Kutaisi entertainment" (1903)	62
3.3	"The last days of Tbilisi's 'Konka' Tramway" (1904)	63
7.1	Coffee grounds before they are tapped	131
7.2	A more balanced heap	132
9.1	The coffee bar, *Kaffebrenneriet*	177
9.2	The coffee bar, *Java*	181
9.3	The coffee bar, *Evita*	182

Contributors

Alex Broom is Associate Professor of Sociology and Australian Research Council Future Fellow, School of Social Science, The University of Queensland, Australia. He specializes in the sociology of traditional, complementary, and alternative medicine (TCAM) and the sociology of cancer and end-of-life care.

Ingeborg Grønning is a PhD Research Fellow in Sociology at the NorwegianUniversity of Science and Technology (NTNU), Department of Sociology and Political Science. She has research interests both in urban sociology and in studies of health and technology.

Neeti Gupta is Senior Business Strategist at Microsoft. She has an MSc from the Massachusetts Institute of Technology. Her research and professional work has allowed her to straddle the worlds of technology and culture, production and consumption, design and user experience to explore experience design in online and offline community.

Keith N. Hampton is Associate Professor of Communication at the Rutgers University. His research interests focus on the relationship between information and communication technologies, social networks, and the urban environment.

Ida Marie Henriksen is a PhD Research Fellow in Sociology at the Norwegian University of Science and Technology (NTNU), Department of Sociology and Political Science. She researches within urban sociology, with special interest in interaction in public and semi-public spaces.

Erling Dokk Holm is Associate Professor of Urbanism at the Oslo School of Management, Norway. His research focuses on the use of urban landscapes and the relationship between economic structural change and identity discourses in an urban setting. Dokk Holm also serves as Dean at the Oslo School of Management.

Eric Laurier is Senior Lecturer in Geography and Interaction at the University of Edinburgh. He has carried out research on sociability and work in cafes, the everyday life of car travel, and the organization of film production during the editing process. His research draws upon ethnomethodology and conversation analysis.

Paul Manning is Associate Professor of Anthropology at the Trent University, Peterborough, Canada, and author of *Semiotics of Drink and Drinking* (Bloomsbury Publishing, 2012). He is also the editor of *Semiotic Review*.

Ray Oldenburg is a Emeritus Professor of Sociology at the University of West Florida, Pensacola, Florida, USA, usually identified as an urbanologist. More properly his concern is with the physical environment and its effects on people's life.

Graham Scambler is Professor of Medical Sociology at the University College London, UK. He is the author or editor of a dozen books on social theory, health and health care, sex work and sport, as well as over a hundred chapters and articles. He is a founding editor of the international journal *Social Theory and Health*. He is an Academician of the Academy of Social Sciences, UK.

Tomas Moe Skjølsvold is a Postdoctoral Research Fellow at the Norwegian University of Science and Technology (NTNU), Department of Interdisciplinary Studies of Culture. His current research projects revolve around issues of energy, sustainability and everyday use of technology, and he is also interested in more general theoretical and empirical sociological explorations.

Bodil Stenseth is a freelance historian and writer, with special interest in "micro-history" and history of mentality. Among her books are the biography *Munch – The Story of a Family*, and most recently *Wergeland Street*, a study of urbanization and urbanism in the city of Oslo 1840–2013.

Aksel Tjora is Professor of Sociology at the Norwegian University of Science and Technology (NTNU), Department of Sociology and Political Science. His research is focused on the interactional production of community in various areas: in organizations, between users of technologies, within health care delivery, in public space, and in relation to city planning and cultural events. Tjora is also the editor of the Norwegian *Journal of Sociology*.

Peter Walters is an urban sociologist from The University of Queensland in Brisbane, Australia. He researches and publishes on urban community and change in the inner city and the outer suburbs. He has recently commenced a collaborative project researching governance and the urban poor in Bangladesh. He also researches agro-forestry and village life in the Solomon Islands, which has nothing to do with cities.

Introduction

Aksel Tjora and Graham Scambler

The café has a special symbolism in modernity, whether the caffeine *fix* is associated with the cities of coffee's origins to the East, the Viennese salons of the late ninteenth century, the 1950s and 1960s Parisian retreats of Sartre and de Beauvoir, the coffee bars of London's Soho, or the current outlets of the profit-sapping and tax-avoiding chains based in contemporary North America. Cafés are everywhere and used even by confirmed tea-drinkers. The café, in other words, is an important social space. This volume explores its parameters, usage, changing role as what Oldenburg (1989) calls a "third place" (as opposed to the first place, the home, and the second place, work), and what it *means* not only to its citizens-cum-consumers but also to those whose labor allow it to be what it is. It is the editors' and contributors' hope that it will be a catalyst for further research and for a more refined theorization of what we characterize as "café society."

The "how's' and 'why's" of the appeal of café spaces by time and place is one theme here. Another is usage and purpose. The third concerns how the café is produced and reproduced as a social institution by the day-to-day actions of its personnel, managers, and baristas as well as customers. And the forth is more reliant on theory than practice: what can, and sometimes does, what we call café society promise for the future? Answers to this family of queries demand a mix of historic, geographic and social methodologies. This collection is a first stab. We have attempted to sample macro-, meso- and microsociology, the editors' home discipline, as well as allied disciplines. The results, as ever, are provisional. Our aspiration is to facilitate a more comprehensive, interdisciplinary approach to the study of the contemporary café, and to hypothesize that many of us—globally as well as locally—now inhabit a *café society*. What might this hypothesis about café society amount to? Is the café of growing salience for civil society as well as a safe haven and site of easy and routine sociability? Is it a de facto candidate as well as a metaphor for what one of us has termed civil society's "enabling sector" (Scambler and Kelleher, 2006)? In short, is it becoming a third place or arena particularly conducive to personal and political resistance to the intrusive or colonizing imperatives of state or class? To suggest so is to pick up on Habermas' (1989) classic account of the role of eighteenth century European cafés as providers of a space allowing for open and uncensored political debate and the "public use of reason," a bastion of (admittedly male, bourgeois) independent-mindedness. Habermas argued a generation ago that these cafés and salons have long since been neutered by an unholy alliance of state and class. Civil society and the public sphere in which it sits are diminished. But are today's cafés recognizable progeny of this European ancestry (do they share its DNA)?

No less intriguing than such 'big' questions are those focusing on the café as a living, organic sociocultural institution. Cafés are now inevitably about *networks* and *connectedness*. From the perspective of some investigators, sentiments of togetherness and belonging are "artful accomplishments," living only as long as they are invested and reinvested with life. Laurier (2005) is one who deploys ethnomethodological theory and ethnographic research to explore how customers, owners, baristas, and others create and recreate the contemporary café as space and institution. The café is for "familiar strangers." It specializes in "familiarity bonds" that can not only give succour but also enhance well-being, quality of life, and maybe even, at a pinch, health and longevity (Scambler and Tjora, 2012). Laurier has examined the practices that bestow these rewards.

So the study of café life encompasses both macro- and microworlds. It also extends beyond any single discipline. Complimenting sociology are lively contributions from

INTRODUCTION 3

historians, economists, geographers, as well as from representatives of the arts and humanities. We have not been able to give each and every perspective a voice of its own in this volume. We have however spanned not only disciplines but also times and places. The authors have delivered a rich, comparative sampling of why references to a café society are not far-fetched but worth pursuing.

Café society, this volume implies, reflects a number of discernible empirical trends:

- a rapidly increasing number of commercially viable cafés across contemporary Western (but not just Western) societies;
- a growing potential for these discrete and "bounded spaces" to serve as third places;
- ready accessibility, extending beyond the affluent to accommodate the non-, un- and under-employed;
- a potential for cafés to be more than sites for sociability or familiarity bonds;
- cafés as spaces for multinetworking, stretching from weak to strong ties;
- cafés as possible resources for the enabling sector of civil society.

In chapter 1, Ray Oldenburg, originator of the concept of the ("great good") third place and catalyst for a renewed interest in the likes of cafés, opens the narrative with a scene-setting account of the multiple facets of hanging out together. He considers the many functions cafés perform. He also hypothesizes that what some deem substitutes for the kind of face-to-face interaction cafés facilitate, like Facebook, will fade out of contention. The café will survive, "especially the one with terrace seating that shows itself to the passing parade as the best that civilization has to offer."

Bodil Stenseth presents a cultural microhistory of "The Living Room," a long-established café in the ever-evolving neighborhood comprising the Majorstuen district of Oslo. As Majorstuen changed, recently by means of its gentrification, so too did its third places. One theme that runs through this contribution is that of cosmopolitanism. The author sees the contemporary café both as emergent from what went before and as a vital site of present-day cosmopolitan belonging.

Chapter 3, by Paul Manning, takes off from Alfred Polgar's seminal "Theory of the Café Central" (1926). His project in this piece is to compare and contrast concepts of the *Café Central* and the *Café Peripheral*. What he offers is a provisional theory of the latter. His route takes him by two cafés in Georgia's Tblisi. The first, *Kimerioni*, he defines as a modernist café, the second, *Laghidze*, as a modernizer's café. He leavens his discussion of the different missions behind these two cafés with a consideration of their actual usage.

Graham Scambler focuses in Chapter 4 on cafés in London, past and present. He offers typologies both of cafés themselves and of the uses people make of them. A major strand in his discussion is the potential cafés represent for third place activity oriented to political resistance. Might the café constitute a kind of "enabling sector" of civil society, a conduit for transmitting activism into its "protest sector"? Does it contain any of the DNA of the eighteenth-century English coffeehouses Habermas (1989) analyzed?

Ida Marie Henriksen, Tomas Moe Skjølsvold, and Ingeborg Grønning report the results of a small empirical study of "people in cafés" conducted in Trondheim, Norway. So Chapter 5 puts some flesh on the skeleton. They distinguish between (a) takeaway customers, (b) regulars, (c) workers, (d) loners, (e) social guests, and (f) mothers. In their conclusion, they ask how a café can both serve multiple functions *and* somehow mesh into a community. The importance of routine, a sense of belonging and "public solitude" underpin their answer.

In Chapter 6, Aksel Tjora takes ethnomethodological steps beyond the works on community of Tönnies and Dürkheim to develop a notion of "communal awareness." Drawing on his own research and observations in four cafés across three continents he identifies five types of communal interaction: "recognizing the other," "experiencing situations together," "perceiving the other's needs," "trusting the other," and "showing and accepting curiosity." These contribute to and result in, he suggests, a subtle form of communal awareness that epitomizes café society.

Eric Laurier builds on his previous body of research to dissect the increasingly symbolic role of the barista in Chapter 7. Drawing also on an ethnomethodological perspective and a personal apprenticeship, he both brings to life and articulates or "makes accessible" the acquisition of practical knowledge and skills that characterize the contemporary barista. This chapter covers a neglected aspect of café society, the role of the worker as opposed to those of the (often corporate) owner or customer.

Chapter 8, by Keith Hampton and Neeti Gupta, was first published in the form of a paper in "New Media and Society" (Vol 10 (6), 2008). We have included it here because it addresses a pivotal issue around café usage: does public/semi-public Wi-Fi use have implications for sociability? Specifically, does wireless Internet use in nonprivate settings act as an impediment to notions of togetherness and community? Their data from Boston and Seattle lead them to distinguish between (a) true mobiles and (b) placemakers.

In Chapter 9, aptly entitled "design for solitude," Erling Dokk Holm explores the relevance and impact of the design and construction of cafés as social spaces for the interaction they host. It draws on original data from a mixed-methods PhD study of three cafés in Oslo. Like many contributions to this volume, it makes more tangible Oldenburg's conceptualization of the third place. Cafés *are* the production and reproduction of people's behaviors; and their physical parameters enable/constrain these behaviors.

The book ends with Peter Walters and Alex Broom's shrewd reflections on café culture in Australia in Chapter 10. Noting the growth and spread of café culture over the last decade, they contend that this adds up to a disaffection with "individualization" and a desire to return to a more communal aesthetic. They make a distinction between the cosmopolitan and communitarian thrusts of the contemporary third place. Emphasizing the significance of sociocultural context and structures or relations like gender, they suggest that the contemporary Aussie café is a kind of litmus paper for the future of the third place.

The chapters that make up this text are as heterogeneous as they are complementary. Together, we maintain, they proffer a synthesis and invitation to further theorize and investigate the idea that a "café society" is emerging, and all that this does or might involve. Cafés are the product of human enterprise even as they shape it, the classic sociological dialectic of agency and structure. Sociologists can and must learn from allied disciplines like anthropology, history, geography, and political science, as well as from the arts, humanities, urban (and rural) planning, architecture, and civil engineering. The core question this collection poses? The café is on the rise: what does this amount to? Does our concept of a "café society," denoting a novel, pervasive and distinctive subculture and third place, amount to more than a passing phase?

References

Habermas, J. (1989) *The Structural Transformation of the Public Sphere: An Enquiry into a Category of Bourgeois Society*. Cambridge: Polity Press.

Laurier, E. (2005) *The Cappucino Community: Cafes and Civic Life in the Contemporary City*. ESRC Final Report. Glasgow: University of Glasgow.

Oldenburg, R. (1989) *The Great Good Place: Cafes, Shops, Community Centres, Beauty Parlours, General Stores, Bars, Hangouts and How They Get You Through the Day*. New York: Paragon House.

Polgar, A. (1926) Theorie des 'Café Central.' English translation in Grafe, C. and Bollerey, F. (Eds) (2007) *Cafes and Bars: The Architecture of Public Display*. Oxford: Routledge.

Scambler, G. and Kelleher, D. (2006) New social and health movements: issues of representation and change. *Critical Public Health*, 16, 1–13.

Scambler, G. and Tjora, A. (2012) 'Familiarity bonds': a neglected mechanism for middle-range theories of health and longevity. *Medical Sociology Online*.

1

THE CAFÉ AS A THIRD PLACE

Ray Oldenburg

The Boston wit, Thomas Appleton, once remarked that "Good Americans, when they die, go to Paris." That aphorism is more appropriate today than it was a century and a half ago for in the interim American cities have been shaped to accommodate automobiles, not people. Paris would be "Heaven" for Americans who, during their lives, suffered the lifeless streets of suburbia and the cold corporate towers of the Central Business Districts and were denied those "long sweet days, of the sidewalk cafés," to paraphrase Joseph Wechsberg (1967). Small wonder that Paris is the most visited city in the world.

In this chapter, we review the concept of the "Third Place" in order that cafés and their contribution to personal and social life might be better understood and more highly valued. The concept of the third place is sometimes introduced as a correction of Freud's contention that emotional well-being depends on having someone to love and work to do (Grossman, 1990). Evidence the world over, however, suggests that beyond the conjugal nest and the work lot there must also be a *third* place. It is "The Great Good Place" described in fiction by Henry James; a haven of rest and recuperation, an escape from the daily grind (James, 1990). There is, however, much more than that to be gained from third place sociability.

What, then, is a "third place?" The concept derives from the advent of the industrial revolution that put considerable distance between the home (the first place) and the workplace (the second place) both in terms of physical and social separation. Both the home and the workplace are relatively small worlds and both constrain individuals to play the social roles those settings require. Those two settings may be said to anchor our lives. Taken together, however, they are adequate neither to the development of community nor to the broadening of the individual. Toward those ends a third place is needed, one in which people from a diversity of backgrounds combine to expand one another's understanding of the world and, out of the bonds formed there, community takes root.

Most third places, but certainly not all, are business establishments that serve food and/or drink to customers on a daily basis. When people from many walks of life visit such places often and for the pleasure of one another's company, it is, for them, a third place. They are the "regulars" (or "habitués" in café parlance) and it is the regulars (i.e. regular visitors), more than staff or management, who set the tone of conviviality within. Their laughter, their banter, their good-natured jibes at one another all combine to make the third place a treasured respite from the cares and concerns of the day. The regulars are not a closed circle. In the usual case, they are proud of the diversity in their number and are always happy to receive a new "member" as doing so promises new things to talk about and to learn.

In seventeenth-century England, a political movement was promoted by the Levellers to eliminate all distinctions in position or rank in order to make everyone equal. It did not succeed in transforming British society, but it did succeed in England's newly evolving coffeehouses where a new intimacy emerged among people who had earlier been kept distant from one another. Two features essential to its success were introduced simultaneously and the first was the low cost of entry and participation. A penny was the price of admission. Two pence was the price of a cup of coffee. A clay pipe cost a penny and a newspaper was free. These coffeehouses sprouted all over London and came to be called "Penny Universities." So popular did they become that the amount of small change minted was inadequate to the demand and the coffeehouses and the houses had to issue tokens that were generally acceptable within the immediate area.

The second feature was that of posting the same set of rules in every coffeehouse, the first lines of which required all persons, regardless of station or position in society, to be treated as equals. This requirement, to the surprise of many, was readily accepted by patrons at all levels and in no small part because of the excitement these places offered in contrast to the highly segregated society in which they existed.

Owing to the remarkable advances in electronic communication, it has become fashionable for many to argue in behalf of "virtual" third places, which one can engage while sitting at his or her computer. That notion, however, abuses the word "virtual," which means that one thing is the same as another in both essence and effect. As Christopher Lasch observed, the difference between face-to-face versus electronic communication is that between participating and being a spectator (Lasch, 1995). One must also consider how "virtual third places" differ from real ones in terms of their formation.

Real third places contain a generous mix of people who happen upon a particular site for a variety of reasons. They *do not* pick the people they associate with in a real third place. But in "virtual third places" that is precisely what happens. Mary Parker Follett addressed the difference many years ago in her discussion of horizontal versus vertical relationships (Follett, 1918). When the individual does the picking as in "virtual third places," the like-minded are brought together. Ms. Follett was not at all impressed with "cosmopolites" who are "all the same." When like-minded people associate, there is very little broadening of experience for the individual. "The satisfaction and contentment that comes with sameness," she said, "indicates a meager personality (Follett, 1918: 196)." The charm of the mix was nicely illustrated years ago by Peter Donald in his description of the mid-day regulars in New York's fashionable Club 21. It was "a kind of luncheon club that never got around to lunch" with eight or ten as a nucleus and "no two in the same racket" and therefore not equipped to bore one another with shop talk. There was a symphony conductor, a lawyer, a jeweler, a carpet tycoon, a steel magnate, a comedian, an ad man, sundry newshawks, and devalued millionaires (Donald, 1950).

Conversation is the main activity in third places. It is characteristically lively and holds the attention of everyone in the circle. This is not because those assembled are great speakers. Three factors contribute to the animated give and take among the membership. First, there is broad latitude for members to introduce almost any subject and to change subjects often. Second, as those present come from different backgrounds, they are more interesting than those the individual lives or works with day in and day out. Third, as the group often brings a half dozen or more people into conversation, one must both wait to talk and to judge one's words carefully when gaining the floor. As Fran Lebowitz once quipped, the opposite of talking is not listening; the opposite of talking is waiting.

Most third places are modest, accessible, and very affordable. For the price of a cup of coffee or a glass of wine or draft beer, one may linger as long as one pleases. Hours of operation are geared to the demands of the first and second places, which means that they may open earlier or stay open later than other businesses.

The Functions of Third Places

With the exception of the *joie de vive* or *la dolce vita* cultures, third places in the Western hemisphere have not enjoyed a good reputation. Both social reformers and urban planners have condemned them. "Hanging out" has been regarded as a small step above loitering. In the United States, the Supreme Court imposed single-use zoning in 1926 allegedly to protect urban residents from all manner of nuisances real and imagined. That judgment, of course, disallowed gathering places in residential neighborhoods where, if community life is to exist, they are needed most.

Third places serve individuals, communities, and the larger society in a variety of ways not widely understood. In considering these, it is well to bear in mind the reciprocity between individuals and their society; that which contributes to the well-being and happiness of the individual makes for a more pleasant and stable society.

Unify the Neighborhood

The closing scene in the movie "Fried Green Tomatoes" shows a weather-beaten Whistle Stop Café closed for business and abandoned. "It's funny how a little place like this brought so many people together" is the last spoken line and apt testimony for the town's one third place. It is important for people who share a locality to know one another; to know who can be counted on for what; to know who the leaders are, who to avoid, and who might become friends. When a place for all those souls to meet and get to know one another exists, there will be the genesis of community.

In areas of the city where cafés, diners, and coffee shops coexist with a variety of other businesses, it is common for the former to open their doors an hour or so before the other places of business. This allows local business men to meet there and keep in touch the better to serve themselves and their customers.

Friends by the Set

Among the more obvious, and to the individual more important, functions of a third places is the provision of a set of friends. In the words of Pete Hamill:

> To hang out is a special thing. There is no specific way to define the experience but everyone who has done it knows what it is all about. It means, first of all, that you have friends. The friends are, as always, friends in spite of, not because of. They will not advance your career, or sell you insurance late at night, or try to steal your woman. They understand that at its dark secret root friendship is a conspiracy...But aside from friends...there must also be a place. (Hamill, 1969)

For those who thus enjoy the regular company of friends, the third place is indeed a blessing as it solves the major problem of having friends, which is sometimes called the Paradox of

Friendship. Simply stated, we like our friends, we enjoy being with our friends, but we don't want them "in our hair." As Richard Sennett put it, "...people can be sociable only when they have some protection from one another (Sennett, 1977). When friends meet at a third place, they may arrive and depart as it pleases them individually.

The average adult, we are told, has between three and five close friends and numbers are important here. A longitudinal study done in California some years ago demonstrated that the chances of living a long and satisfying life depend on the number of friends one has (Berkman and Syme, 1979). Seven thousand subjects were matched for initial health, health practices, obesity, smoking, drinking, and social class and then sorted into age and gender groups and into categories based on the number of friends each subject could claim. In all cases, longevity increased as the number of friends increased. For example, only 9.6 percent of the men aged 50–59 and who were "most connected" were dead nine years later as compared to 30.8 percent of the "least connected." Among women aged 50–69, 9.7 percent of the "most connected" had died as compared to 29.4 percent of the "least connected."

Those who have a third place and visit it regularly have an advantage both in the number of friends acquired and time spent with them. Those who opt for allegiance to a third place also gain a source of satisfaction that is unique in its singularity. If we compare third place involvement with involvement in home life and that in the workplace in terms of relationships with significant others, we find that spouses are the greatest source of satisfaction in the lives of married people, but they are also a source of conflict. If we examine the work situation, we find that bosses are a major source of conflict. The third place offers satisfaction without conflict.

The Joys of Camaraderie

In his tribute to places to hang out, Pete Hamill also commented on the differences between his colleagues, remarking that: "The most stopped-up, intellectually constipated, and unhappy men I know are those who work all day and go straight home to eat, watch TV, and sleep. There is no special period of the day reserved for the company of other men, no private experiences outside of work and marriage" (Hamill, 1969: 311). The place to hang out in England is the pub and a research team back in the 1940s identified it as

> the only kind of public building used by large numbers of people where their thoughts and actions are not in some way being arranged for them; in the other kinds of public buildings they are the audiences, watchers of political, religious, dramatic, cinematic, instructional, or athletic spectacles. But within the four walls of the pub, once a man has bought or been bought his glass of beer, he has entered an environment in which he is participator rather than spectator. (Mass Observation, 1943)

John Mortimer, through his character Rumpole, highlights the importance of camaraderie in an episode where Rumpole is about to lose a comrade to marriage. He implores his friend to think of "those peaceful moments of the day. Those hours we spend with a bottle of Chateau Fleet Street, from 5:30 on, in Pomeroy's Wine Bar. That wonderful oasis of peace that lies between the battle of the Bailey and the horrors of Home Life" (Mortimer, 1981).

Typically though, the third place is hardly a peaceful oasis when the gang is gathered in full number and the revelry begins. At one point in our investigations, we had 33 groups of people observed in third place settings. The parties varied in number from three to eight persons per table or booth, and they were observed for three minutes each. The total of 148 people laughed 792 times. Doing a little arithmetic, we calculated that the average person laughed at the rate of 107 times per hour in these third place settings. This is rather striking when seen against the number of times the average American is reported to laugh per day and that figure varies between 17 and 20 (Feinberger and Mead, 1980). Laughter, we are told, increases our energy, increases blood flow, lowers blood pressure, and reduces stress. It also strengthens the bonds between people who laugh together. As Victor Borge once put it, "The shortest distance between two people is laughter."

What gives rise to all this laughter? It is not jokes for they are a second-hand form of humor and many who love to laugh don't like jokes at all. Indeed, the third place regular never comes closer to being a bore as when he tells a joke. Much third place humor plays on being impolite in a manner that really communicates affection. It is often heard when a regular enters and sees a buddy: "Oh no! If I'd known you were here I'd have kept on going." And a rejoinder: "Can't you find anyone else to bother?" Or to the bartender: "What kind of a place are you running here?" Such remarks are only made when there are others to hear them.

Revelry typically reaches its peak in all-male settings where working men are gathered and alcohol is served. In Canada, before the brasseries began offering quieter and more genteel settings, the old-fashioned, all male, beer only taverns hosted immodest beer consumption and boisterousness where noisy arguments, yelling, and shouting were encouraged. Men went there to "whoop it up," but there were well-understood limits.

There were large tables at which patrons had to remain seated; they were not allowed along the bar. Profanity was not allowed. Drunks were promptly evicted. The beer was served by male waiters old enough to have been around and big enough to play the bouncer. There were no gimmicks or "draws" beyond beer and the opportunity to vent one's opinion in strong voice.

One might question the need for such places. We talked one day with a psychiatrist all too familiar with wife-beating, and he attributed most of it to the lack of neighborhood taverns where men used to go to "let off steam." We have no doubt they served that function as well as many others.

An Intellectual Forum

Normally one thinks of intellectualism in bookish terms. Yet "the capacity for learning and understanding" is broader than that. One of the most important achievements of the intellect is to gain an understanding and appreciation of the other human beings who share our environment. It is this broadening of understanding that third place involvement makes possible. It is the unplanned mix of occupations, ethnic backgrounds, geographic origins, travel experiences, and class positions that enrich one's understanding of the human condition. One learns by reading a book, but one learns differently in face-to-face interaction, in participating in the give-and-take of socializing with a goodly mix of friends and acquaintances. Much more is communicated than is put into words.

In recent times, the third place has become an intellectual forum in a manner that more readily appeals to our notion of what an intellectual setting might be. A revolution of sorts has taken place in the business world where it was once thought that productivity increased as a function of the amount of time employees remained at their desks. All that has changed for most knowledge workers these days as both where one works and when one works is increasingly left to the workers. Collaboration has become the mantra and the solitary office has given way to settings that encourage lively conversation and interaction, which hastens innovation and "thinking outside the box." Places that offer coffee and laptop facilities are favored.

With cafés in mind, we would be remiss not to mention that so many of them are visited with books to be read and, in a good many instances, books to be written. Cafés, unlike pubs, bars, and taverns invite long and leisurely visits in which a book is often an excellent companion.

A Port of Entry

It is a sad fact of life in American suburbs that a new resident has no occasion and no place to meet the neighbors. What greets the new resident, as the architect Raymond Curran has pointed out is a residential creation characterized by personal isolation and independence from a communal context (Curran, 1983). Before single-use zoning contaminated the land, there was usually a place on the corner, a tavern, a grocery, a drugstore, or whatever where people met one another on a daily basis. There a newcomer could quickly learn what the neighborhood contained; where to get what and who could be helpful in one way or another

Where local businesses exist amid the houses and apartments in which people reside, the newcomer usually gets announced to the older residents by the merchants who are always curious about new customers and, in their own ways, find out about them. Thus the newcomer becomes known to the neighborhood with very little effort on his part. One can see here, the importance of local "Mom and Pop" stores to the creation and maintenance of community.

A Staging Area

When Hurricane Andrew struck Southern Florida many able-bodied men walked out of their homes eager to lend help to those who needed it. The problem was that most of them had no idea where to go to meet others as their neighborhoods were developed without any places where neighbors might meet. The lack of places where people might congregate in emergency situations may seem trivial to some, but it should be borne in mind that it takes a lot of time for officialdom to respond to emergencies and time is most often of the essence.

Generating Social Capital

In the business world, individuals succeed in no small way as a function of the number of friends they has. Similarly, towns, cities, and counties succeed in large part as a function of the bonds of trust and understanding existing between their citizens. These ties that are formed between people in a given area are called social capital and the more social capital accumulates, the better the area does economically. Those who study the formation of social capital distinguish between "bridging" and "bonding" ties. When social networks are based on some important criterion common to all members of the network (when people are *alike* in some way), that is bonding. When the members of a network are not alike, they form bridging ties.

Most networks contain both bridging and bonding ties but one must suspect that third places generate more bridging ties because it is the mere proximity of place that draws most of their regulars to them. In the United States, particularly in the "Old South," there are many counties where the sale of and consumption of alcohol in public is prohibited.

These are called "dry" counties, and they generate less social capital than the "wet" counties wherein many of the third places sell alcohol for consumption on the premises.

Mutual Aid Societies

When "the gang" gets together in their third place, any member who needs help with something has long since learned that this is the place to mention it. Between them the regulars know a great many people with a great many skills and a good deal of knowledge. Out of these connections plumbers, carpenters, electricians, and other craftsmen are obtained at reduced rates. In one group, a member's Oldsmobile needed a new alternator and one of the other guys went outside and put in a rebuilt one in a matter of minutes. In another case, a tree had to come down in one of the chap's backyard and a friend in the group was out there next day with his chainsaw. Tools and other equipments are loaned and items no longer wanted by one member are gladly received by another. The cost of living is reduced when one is a member of a group of good friends and in the usual case, the matter of who owes who never comes up.

It is also typical, when a member of the group doesn't show up for two days in a row for one of the group to drop by his or her place to see if anything is the matter. Though items may pass from one member to another, gifts are not given and birthdays are usually ignored, particularly in men's groups.

Adding Life to the Public Domain

An increasing problem in the cities of the world's most advanced societies is that of making the public domain more hospitable. As cities are planned more for automobiles than pedestrians, as the pace of life quickens, and as the people who work downtown can't afford to live there, cities lose the vitality they had a century ago. Many cities are moving toward a remedy by permitting the private, for profit, use of public space. They are promoting the development of sidewalk cafés not only by issuing permits for the private use of public space but also by making the approval process easier and by allowing the use of outdoor space heaters to increase the months of operation. New York city that once disallowed open sidewalk cafés now has nearly a thousand of them with about 80 percent of them in Manhattan.

It was common for cities to have laws prohibiting sidewalk cafés or restaurants for health reasons and those were established in horse and buggy days when livery stables begot high piles of manure and germ-carrying flies were everywhere. This may have retarded the emergence of sidewalk cafés somewhat and, if so, that is unfortunate for it is hard to imagine an amenity that does more to make the city a human habitat than the sidewalk café.

Sidewalk cafés lend many advantages to a city. They put "eyes on the street" that not only makes for a human environment but also lessens crime. There is no police force in the world big enough to keep city streets safe all the time. Safe streets are maintained by the substantial number of people who use them and provide a "natural surveillance" over what goes on in them. Similarly, it is the regulars of a third place who become highly familiar not only with the place they visit but also with the area surrounding it and they are always alert to anything that shouldn't be there.

Sidewalk cafés increase business along the streets where they are located and beyond that, they increase the income of these cafés as competition among them grows. We saw this in a California city some years ago. On a tour of West Hollywood in the early 90s, we noticed that Sunset Strip had several sidewalk cafés all of which looked filled to the maximum. Our guide explained that one restaurateur had tried and succeeded with it only to discover that he did better after a nearby competitor copied him, and better yet when more were added. They had made the strip the place to be—a place for people to gather and socialize, to see and be seen. More recently, the same pattern obtained in Walla Walla, Washington where all the adjacent businesses are doing better with about a dozen sidewalk cafés having given life to the downtown area. Leisurely visits to those cafés have made residents aware of interesting downtown shops they never knew existed.

The emergence of sidewalk cafés is an example, in many areas, of the pedestrian finally gaining ground against the automobile in city planning and with the success they are enjoying it may be predicted that two other trends will follow: widening of the sidewalks and the restriction of automobile traffic.

The Contribution to Democracy

John Dewey once noted, "the heart and final guarantee of democracy is in the free gatherings of neighbors on the street corners to discuss back and forth and converse freely with one another" (Dewey, 1976). More than the street corners that offer no seating and no protection from the weather, it is in third places where people sit "solving the problems of the world." The mix of people and their differing points of view serve as a hedge against the possibility that one may become an ideologue, smug, and self-satisfied in one's certitudes and incapable of seeing the other sides of issues. In the United States, the main variants are the conservative and liberal viewpoints, and more and more people get their political "insights" from television. There the highly slanted offerings from the left or the right are offered without criticism and accepted as true by the majority.

Still, the third place contributes to a democratic society by countering the excesses of ideology. The differing points of view expressed there encourage thinking. The groans someone gets when expressing a "hair-brained idea" encourages mental discipline and discourages those for whom belief trumps knowledge.

Grass roots democracy also depends on the residents of a given locality to have considerable input into what happens in the neighborhood and that depends on the residents having the places and the occasions to meet and discuss matters of mutual interest. Unfortunately, this ideal is not realized in most large cities where the residents are involved neither in the planning nor the ongoing development of their neighborhoods.

Summing Up

The foregoing list of functions performed by most third places is not exhaustive. Social change is ongoing and so are the places and the benefits they provide. The American taverns and the pubs of the British Isles are fading as are French cafés. The most inclusive American third place ever was the soda fountain and it is near extinction. On the other hand, libraries and churches are being redesigned more and more to provide the third place experience and coffee shops are on the rise.

There are notions afloat these days that would appear to reduce or even eliminate the need for third places such as the idea that "Facebook" can give us scores of real friends or that sitting at one's computer can put one in a third place. These ideas will fade and the importance of face-to-face interaction has never been greater, and it, of course, requires places where people may gather and indulge themselves in the spirit of geniality. Chief among these places, in this writer's view, is the café and especially the one with terrace seating that shows itself to the passing parade as the best civilization has to offer.

References

Berkman, L. and Syme, S. L. (1979) Social networks, host resistance, and mortality: a nine-year follow-up study of Almeda County residents. *American Journal of Epidemiology*, 109, 2, 186–204.

Curran, R. J. (1983) *Architecture and the Urban Experience*. New York: Van Nostrand Reinhold Co.

Dewey, J. (1976) Creative Democracy: The Task Before Us. In Boyston, J. (Ed.) *John Dewey: The Later Works, 1925–1953*. Vol. 14. Carbondale: Southern Illinois University Press (Original work published 1030), 224–230.

Donald, P. (1950) Gentlemen Songsters. in *The Iron Gate*. New York: The Jack Krindler Foundation.
Feinberger, M. and Mead, W. R. (1980) *American Averages Garden City*. New York: Dolphin Books.
Follett, M. P. (1918) *The New State*. Longman: Green & Co.
Grossman, R. (1990, February) Hangouts. *The Chicago Tribune*.
Hamill, P. (1969, November) A Hangout is a Place...*Mademoiselle*, p 151.
James, H. (1990, January) The great good place. *Scribner's Magazine*.
Lasch, C. (1995) *The Revolt of the Elites*. New York: W.W. Norton and Company.
Mass Observation (1943) *The Pub and the People: A Worktown Study*. London: Victor Gollanca Ltd.
Mortimer, J. (1981) Rumpole and the Man of God. In *The Trials of Rumpole*. New York: Penguin Books.
Sennett, R. (1977) *The Fall of Public Man*. New York: Alfred A Knopf.
Wechsberg, J. (1967, August) The long sweet day of the Sidewalk café. *Holiday Magazine*.

2

Heart of Urbanism. The Café: A Chapter of Cultural History

Bodil Stenseth

Early one morning, Birgit locks the door of her apartment behind her and strolls over to "The Living Room," her local café, located just a couple of blocks away. Devoid of make-up, she is wearing knock-around clothes, that is, sneakers, jeans, and a sweater, topped by an all-weather jacket with pockets big enough to accommodate her laptop. Once inside, she perks up to the smell of freshly ground coffee and the sputter of the espresso machine behind the counter. The Living Room is small and intimate, just like home. It offers neither designer chairs nor tables of glass and steel, but rather an eclectic collection of living room furniture that had seen better days before arriving at the local school's flea market. The day's tabloid newspapers and some very well-thumbed magazines are spread out across the high, narrow table in front of the wall-to-wall picture window.

That very same window is reputed to have once framed mannequins clad in Norwegian-made ladies' wear. After the ladies' clothing store closed, Tove signed a lease on the store and opened a café there, where the window now serves as a transparent wall against the city. Café guests who sit on the high bar stools at the table by the window can see and be seen by passers-by on the sidewalk. Birgit does not usually sit there, preferring instead a corner of the sofa in the very back of the café. At this early hour, she can usually have the sofa all to herself. She shares a passing acquaintance with the small group of solitary guests who stop by the café at this hour. She always exchanges a few pleasantries with Peter, Tove's ruggedly handsome assistant. They chat about today's headlines, last night's TV documentary, and a variety of other things. They also have time for a bit of gossip about the neighbors while Birgit leans against the counter as Peter makes her double caffè latte and arranges her ciabatta with mozzarella and tomato on a plate.

Birgit then retires to "her" corner of the sofa that she shares, from time to time, with another freelance writer like herself. She eats her breakfast and makes a half-hearted start on her office work. She reads her usual online newspapers and her email, and then spends some time on Facebook before opening the book review she started to write yesterday. An hour or two pass before she powers down the laptop. On her way out, she takes a minute to chat about the weather with Peter, and then heads for home to continue her working day.

"The Third Place"

Birgit's morning ritual could have played out in Washington DC, Tel Aviv or Copenhagen. That being said, her regular haunt is located in the capital city of Norway. More to the point, it is located at Majorstuen, an affluent West End neighborhood in Oslo. Nearly every weekday morning, she stops by the Living Room, near the apartment in the old building where she lives alone with her cat Nutmeg. The Majorstuen district is home to a myriad of cafés, and Birgit stops at others occasionally, but the Living Room holds a very special place in her heart.

My contribution to this book is based on the premise that cafés constitute the very heart of urbanism today. They are places where neighborhood inhabitants feel at home outside their own homes, where they are "seen" and recognized by others. My term "heart of urbanism" is inspired by a nestor of American sociology—Ray Oldenburg. In his book *The Great Good Place* (1999), he introduced the concept of "the third place" (confer also Chapter 1). In a contemporary urban community, this holds a special meaning since such places are based on individuals' own voluntary and social needs.

The "first place" is defined as the household and the "second place" as the workplace. A "third place" is conductive to community-building in an informal setting. It can be a café, a coffeehouse, a park, or, for that matter, a street corner. Third places promote interaction and bonding between individuals who do not necessarily know each other from school or work, nor have they ever necessarily entered each other's homes. According to Oldenburg, who published a sequel entitled *Celebrating the Third Place* (2001), third places are anchors of community life that facilitate and foster broader, more creative interaction. They nourish a community's social vitality and help promote a functioning democracy.

One explanation for why cafés play such a prominent role in contemporary urban life can be found in the status of the household. There is a clear tendency in the Western world, as well as in the Middle East and Africa, for households to consist of just one single person. In Oslo, in stark contrast to what was the case in the past, more than half of all apartments now constitute single-person households. This has given the café a new and expanded role in people's everyday lives. Since the household has lost a large part of its social and economic significance, the café has taken over some of the traditional functions of the family, thus helping to expand the gap between private and public space.

This chapter has been written from the perspective of microhistory. I try to trace the history of the café, that is, the eighteenth century European café, at Majorstuen, the part of the city where I have lived for nearly 20 years. My household is located on Jacob Aalls gate, one of Majorstuen's longest streets. In 1927, when No. 13—where I live—stood ready to accommodate its first inhabitants, Oslo was rapidly expanding into this area, subsuming it as a kind of satellite village. Since I am a historian and have written a "biography" of No. 13 (Stenseth, 2010). I am fairly well versed in how modern urbanization transformed the lives of those who live and have lived in the building and in the neighborhood.

This chapter is also about cosmopolitanism. Majorstuen is home to flourishing, widely diverse café life. By studying the café, which represents the imposition of a foreign tradition on the West End of Oslo, a small capital city on the periphery of Europe, I hope to facilitate some modicum of understanding about the role of cosmopolitanism in today's city-based world.

The Neighborhoods of Majorstuen

A brief historic description of Majorstuen should be a good place to start. This part of Oslo was established in the late ninteenth century. At the time, it was on the outer perimeter of the city, and it was a traffic hub for street cars, the underground and buses. Later, when road traffic took over the city, one of the Oslo's main thoroughfares was built right through Majorstuen. The city planners laid out a grid pattern for the streets in the new urban area, then added three country roads that had existed since ancient times. The streets were equipped with easements that determined which city blocks would accommodate buildings that housed shops, bars, and restaurants.

The "downtown" sector of the urban district became home to countless small shops. It was in this area where No. 13 was built in 1927, although several four- and five-story apartment buildings had been erected there as early as in the 1890s. There were shops on the ground floors of many of the buildings. The most prominent shops, that is, the apothecaries and grocery shops, usually occupied spacious corner locations. Merchants often leased premises from the building owners, just like the residents in the apartments over the shops. While some apartments were of luxurious proportions, others were somewhat smaller, and still others were very small indeed. At Majorstuen, the upper, middle, and working classes all lived on one and the same block. Back then, private contractors managed to do something that modern city planners can only dream of; they built neighborhoods where people from every social class lived side by side.

The new urban district eventually got its own primary school, church, and sports stadium, as well as several cinemas, banks, and post offices. The area also accommodated numerous workshops and factories, large and small alike. The fact that the population of Majorstuen comprised such a mélange of social classes was ascribable, not least, to the presence of industry and good public transportation. The old tradition of people living close to their workplaces was important far into the twentieth century. Moreover, most of those apartment dwellers were young and not quite so young people who had moved to the city from other parts of Norway. The majority of these "immigrants" had moved from the Norwegian countryside and from towns fairly close to the capital city. For these newcomers, "café" was a foreign word, and many of them were new to life in the big city. Although the Norwegian capital had a population of just 250,000 in the 1920s, it deserved to be called a big city, or perhaps more appropriately, a little big city.

The development of Majorstuen as an urban district was by and large completed in the 1920s. In the post-World War II era, when the city boundaries were expanded and new suburban villages popped up, Majorstuen became an integral part of Oslo's central business district (cf Suarez, 1991).

As far as Majorstuen is concerned, the cityscape of today is basically the same as it was in the 1920s. German tourists enjoy visiting Majorstuen because it reminds them of Berlin in the old days. Many of the architects who were actively designing apartment buildings in about 1900 had been educated in Germany. However, the architect who designed No. 13 and several of the other apartment buildings in the neighborhood belonged to a generation inspired by the urban architecture of the USA. That is, they espoused late Classicism and early Functionalism.

The blocks of apartment buildings have remained almost completely intact at Majorstuen. This is true despite the fact that the area has undergone an extensive makeover during the past 40 years. That being said, many would contend that Majorstuen has lost its distinctive character. It has become cosmopolitan and the population has become more homogeneous. The well-educated middle class dominates, meaning that Majorstuen has been subject to gentrification. While some of the area's old factories have been converted into offices, many have been torn down to make space for shopping centers, office complexes, and apartment buildings. However, many of the ground floor shops have been preserved. There are still small shops there that are family owned and operated, but they are mainly on the side streets these days. In the main street, Bogstadveien, the small shops were taken over by global chains and fast food eateries ages ago and, more recently, cafés have begun to gain ground, quite literally.

Life in Artistic Circles and Café Life

According to the 1927 edition of the Oslo address directory, Majorstuen had three cafés: "The Majorstuen Café," "The Majorstuen Tea Room and Café," and "The Temperance Café" (for teetotallers only). While they were indeed cafés, they were hardly very fashionable ones. We know little about them today, other than that they tended to be located near the end of the line for the street cars. In the old days, there was one famous hospitality venue there: "The Majorstuen Restaurant," which also served as a café, but it was closed down when Oslo's first subway line was built. The restaurant/café was located in a rustic wooden building with a traditional Norwegian rose-painted interior. In addition, it had an outdoor serving area in the courtyard. There were many artists and members of the *literati* among its regular patrons. It was precisely this type of people, that is, rather worldly, sophisticated and familiar with cafés from their travels on the Continent, who must be said to have been the avant-garde of café life.

In the 1800s, life in artistic circles and café life were closely related. Hence the expression "artists' café," exemplified not least when the Grand Café opened in the Norwegian capital in 1867. The café was, and still is, located on Karl Johan, Oslo's parade street. In 1891, when Norway's first international celebrity, Henrik Ibsen, moved back to Kristiania (as Oslo was named until 1925), after many decades on the Continent, the Grand Café became his haunt of preference.

Twice a day he strolled from his home to the Grand, where he had a regular table. He even had his own chair that was officially "Reserved for Dr Ibsen." His daily constitutions up and down Karl Johan Street ultimately turned into something of an attraction. It is said that Ibsen was so punctual that people could set their clocks by him.

From 12.30 to 2.00 p.m., Ibsen took his lunch, consisting of open-faced sandwiches on rolls, beer, and a shot. Afterwards, he would retire to the café's reading room, where there were always fresh newspapers from Norway and abroad. Ibsen's second visit of the day to the Grand Café took place from 6.00 to 7.30 p.m. In the early evening, he liked to have a drink and peruse the newspapers in the reading room in more detail. The rather meticulous Ibsen must have been annoyed by the café's other regular patrons on numerous occasions. The lifestyle of the Kristiania Bohème, an infamous circle of artists and writers, was far from as civil as Ibsen's. Otherwise, both Ibsen and the members of the Kristiania Bohème can still be studied "in situ" today, immortalized in an immense mural on the back wall of the café.

Opened in 1900, the Theatre Café became another favorite haunt of artists. The walls are covered with portraits of writers, painters, and actors. Naturally, some of the artists used their regular tables for writing or to do their office work. Like the Grand Café, the Theatre Café was built in the grand style of the eighteenth century European café. I am referring here to the premier cafés such as Café des Westens in Berlin, Café de Flore in Paris, and Café Central in Vienna (cf. Hjort, 1996).

Oslo's two artists' cafés were, and still are, in the "café Chantal" tradition. However, while a lone pianist entertains café patrons today, there may well have been a string trio in the past. Both the Theatre Café and the Grand Café are still popular hospitality venues in Oslo, although the groups of artists of days past have been superseded by business people, groups of friends, families, and tourists.

Meanwhile, Majorstuen was in the process of developing into a traffic hub, and café life and the cosmopolitan lifestyle took more time to gain foothold there. There may have been several reasons for this. Many of the local residents were used to living in larger, multimember households, and they were unfamiliar with café life. Granted, there were a fair number of single individuals, often referred to as "single lodgers," who rented rooms in the homes of strangers. However, they were rarely people of means and they generally patronized dining halls and self-service restaurants; there were many such eateries at Majorstuen.

The fanciest place to eat at Majorstuen was the Valkyrien Restaurant, which resembled a Parisian sidewalk café and featured a dining hall on the first floor. Soon after the Valkyrien Restaurant opened its doors in 1928, Majorstuen was dubbed "Little Paris." There was a fair amount of bustling traffic in the area, and the blocks located near the trams and subways were dotted with reasonably priced restaurants, bakeries, and tearooms, complemented by a host of small shops.

A Community of Small Shops

Perhaps the most important reason that cafés took such a long time to gain popularity at Majorstuen was the fact that times were tough. The 1920s heralded the onset of a prolonged financial crisis. In the autumn of 1930, the crash on Wall Street reached Oslo, leaving in its wake bankruptcies, standstills—not least in the building industry—and extremely high unemployment. People moved out of city, to neighboring suburbs and towns where the cost of living was lower.

My book on No. 13 documents how severely the Great Depression impacted the households of Majorstuen. The apartment building was home to eight middle-class families at that time. Most of the households consisted of a married couple with children, where the man was usually the family's sole breadwinner. In the devastating crisis that struck in the fall of 1930, one father after the next lost his job. In one of the households in No. 13, a wife had to take on more piano students so that the family could make ends meet. Another household squeezed the family together and rented out several rooms to lodgers. Granted, some households remained unphased by the crisis. One of them was the household of an elderly lady who taught at the local primary school. She was a spinster who lived with her aging mother and an older sister who kept house for them.

In fact, it was probably the local women at Majorstuen who weathered the years of crisis best. These ladies had grown up in a culture that tied most women to the home. To them, extravagance was visiting a tea room or going to the cinema. Cafés and restaurants were and continued to be male strongholds. It says something that as late as in the 1970s, the regular patrons at the Valkyrien Restaurant, Majorstuen's 'Parisian' sidewalk café, were exclusively men.

Meanwhile, the housewives and working women of Majorstuen had their favorite venues—third places—in the local neighborhood. The third places were often small shops, usually run by a husband and wife, two sisters, or a single female merchant. Many of the shops existed for a very long time, longer, in fact, than their proprietors. Majorstuen's small shops included a delicatessen, an apothecary, a butcher, a button shop, a green grocer, a hardware store, a florist, and an electrical shop, as well as a tobacconist and a shop that sold ladies' wear. At the end of every row of houses, there was a corner shop, usually one that sold groceries. In other words, Majorstuen was like a village within the city. The small shops not only met all possible household needs, each of them also formed the framework for a close-knit community within a neighborhood.

Private merchants and specialty shops, traditional gender roles and the Great Depression all played a part in ensuring that the café was not the very heart of urbanism. In point of fact, the heart of urbanism revolved around women's daily ritual of doing the marketing and running their errands at a number of their regular shops.

Milk Instead of Coffee

The evolution of local dairy shops into an institution in the city can be explained by several contemporary notions about what contributed to good health, as well as family patterns and the way in which milk was sold. In the early 1900s, the Norwegian state was in the vanguard of a grand-scale campaign to encourage people to drink milk. The intention was to spread knowledge to the general public about milk as a source of good nutrition, packed with vitamins, proteins, and minerals.

For that reason, the first chapter of the textbook written by Inga Høst and Ingeborg Milberg (1916) used to teach food science in primary schools as from 1916, and whose eighteenth and final edition was published in 1962, extolled milk and all its virtues. School children also learned how they could smell milk to tell whether it was fresh, or whether it was off or sour. Modern housewives needed to know such things. It was not uncommon for a housewife to attend homemaking school as a young girl, where food and good health were at the top of the agenda.

The wise housewife strived to ensure that the whole family, especially the children, drank milk every day. The milk campaign was a success. Even before World War II, Norway's health care authorities could boast impressive statistics, showing that Norwegians had become the biggest milk drinkers in Europe. That being said, it is not known whether milk outcompeted coffee as the drink of choice for the masses— or even whether that was an explicit goal. The eighteenth edition of the food science textbook from 1962 still warned children about the evils of coffee drinking. "Coffee should not be served to children under the age of 16," it said. Coffee 'abuse', that is, drinking too many cups of coffee instead of eating, was also identified as an issue.

The number of dairy shops in a neighborhood appears to have been directly proportionate to the number of large families living in the apartments in the local area. That is, the dairy shops were most common in Majorstuen's working class neighborhoods, where families still traditionally had many children. Yet even in blocks dominated by middle-class families with just one or two children, dairy shops abounded. In 1946, the first year of peace, when milk could once again flow freely and was no longer rationed, Oslo had a record number of dairy shops.

As a rather curious fact, I can add that there was even a Milk Bar that served a variety of milk drinks and cream porridge. In 1936, the Milk Bar opened right in the middle of Oslo's parade street, Karl Johan, not far from the Grand Café. The Milk Bar lasted for about 15 years before being superseded by the café. Meanwhile, it was by no means uncommon for the city's larger retail dairy outlets to have cafés. At Majorstuen, it worked out very well for the "Valkyrien Dairy" to have "N. Johansen's Tea Room" right next door. The dairy supplied the café with cream. In Norway, coffee was customarily served either with or without cream. Coffee was either brewed or percolated, and that was it. It was only in the last two decades of the twentieth century that coffee became more cosmopolitan or sophisticated in Oslo, that is, that coffee became a value-added product.

Home—A Sense of Place

The white beverage was stored in huge milk pails that were kept on ice in the dairy shops' purpose-built basins. Milk was not ordinarily sold in bottles until after World War II. Before that, milk was generally sold by weight or volume, and customers brought their own buckets or jugs when they came to the shop. Regardless of whether they were upper-class wives in their finery, maids, or little girls, everyone had to wait while the milk lady measured out milk or cream. The waiting time often afforded the women an opportunity for a chat. When there was a line at the counter, it was only natural that the regulars were served first. Regular patrons could also charge their purchases, and possibly even get a small discount on everything they bought. Bread, flour, and margarine were conveniently available at the dairy shops. The regulars were even offered certain goods at old prices when there were price hikes.

In No. 13, the ground-floor dairy shop served as the refrigerator for the whole building. Modern electric refrigerators were very costly, and old-fashioned iceboxes were really only prevalent among upper-class households. In the middle and working classes, housewives had to make do with good old-fashioned larders or pantries, where milk did not last long in the summer. For most women, the daily trip to the dairy shop was a ritual. Needs and loyalty usually went hand in hand.

A smart milk lady could certainly make a decent living from running a shop. This was indeed the case with Miss Ølnæs, who set up the dairy shop in No. 13 when the building was new in 1927. She ran it for 30 years, despite a great deal of competition almost on her doorstep. Her secret was that she cleverly cultivated the art of creating a good ambience in the shop, and she chatted about things that she knew would be of interest to the various individual customers. This enabled the milk lady to bond with her customers, winning their loyalty. Thus the dairy shop turned into an informal meeting place for the regular patrons, making it a social space that was an extension of their own homes.

It is, after all, the ambience that makes us see a neighborhood as home. The Norwegian cultural anthropologist Marianne Gullestad, who won international acclaim for her study of everyday life entitled *Kitchen-Table Society*, addressed this topic already in her first work. Her dissertation about an old working-class neighborhood in Bergen was published in book form in 1979. In it, Gullestad ascertained that relationships between people, and the interaction between people and the buildings and streets that envelope them, are crucial to people's well-being. In reality, the grocery shop on the corner played a key role in the lives of the local residents in this particular district in Bergen.

According to Gullestad (1979), this implies that residents of a neighborhood develop a variety of ways to use buildings and streets and ways of dealing with each other, and that these aspects become part of their life pattern and culture. The home environment also gives residents common ground, quite literally, and not least a set of cultural morés to live by.

A grocery shop, a dairy shop, or a café can, in fact, become a cornerstone in people's everyday lives. Such an institution encompasses a finely meshed network of social conventions, relationships, and values. The people who patronized the old dairy shop in No. 13 shared "something," and that "something," I would contend, applies to many people in the heart of today's communities too—through the modern-day café. It gives people a sense of belonging to a place. In many respects, the café has quite recently taken over the traditional role of the dairy shop as the heart of urbanism. Being a regular at a particular café implies connecting and bonding with people in your neighborhood. Every time you enter the venue, you are seen, and those who see you, often know a lot about you.

The Death of the Small Shop

Nearly 100 years after Majorstuen was incorporated into the city of Oslo, the old sense of Majorstuen being a "village" is also history. With few exceptions, the small shops in the neighborhood have closed their doors for good. Shopping malls and global chains have taken their place. John Londei calls the phenomenon *Shutting Up Shop*, and he has documented it admirably in his book of photographs (2007). Shutting up shop is a well-known phenomenon from cities all over the Western World. And wherever small shops still exist in the old neighborhood blocks, their days are probably numbered.

Londei began photographing the small shops, each with its own specialty, in his local neighborhood in London in the 1970s. His book contains pictures of 60 shops, accompanied by portraits of the owner(s) and often also of the shop assistant(s). "Just as important as the shops were the shopkeepers," Londei writes in his introduction, continuing: "To these people running the shop meant so much more than a business. Somehow it felt as if they'd turned the premises into living entities, and they themselves were cherished and long serving members of the community. And how proud they were to still be serving it!"

It was in the late 1960s that Norwegian newspapers began to write about the death of the small shop in Oslo. By then, the dairy shop in No. 13 had been history for quite some time. When Miss Ølnæs passed away, there was no new milk lady to take her place. Shops like hers were no longer viable. With the advent of bottled milk, the grocery stores began to sell it. Bottles called for expensive investments in refrigeration. At

Majorstuen, the last dairy shop closed in the winter of 1979, and it was probably one of the last ones in Oslo.

A journalist who covered the event chatted with some of the dairy shop's regular patrons. They were pensioners. Majorstuen had become a part of town where the residents had a high average age. Young people and families with children preferred living in Oslo's modern new suburbs (cf Suarez, 1991). It is indicative of the situation that the town square outside the Valkyrien Dairy with the adjacent tea room was nicknamed "the Widow Park."

Gentrification

Majorstuen gradually became old and worn down, and it was not until the 1980s that the area began to be upgraded and renovated. That marked the onset of gentrification at Majorstuen. Introduced by British sociologist Ruth Glass in 1964, the concept of gentrification has a tarnished reputation at best. According to the Merriam Webster Dictionary, gentrification is the process of renewal and rebuilding that accompanies the influx of middle-class or affluent people into deteriorating areas, often displacing less-affluent residents.

For younger artists and academics, that is, the educated middle class, Majorstuen was "in." They regarded it as romantic to live in the less-than-convenient old apartment buildings, decorating them with posters, house plants. and furniture from IKEA. As time passed, this generation of residents became more affluent, undertaking major renovation projects that enhanced the appraisal value of their apartments. Notwithstanding, gentrification most certainly also benefited the older inhabitants of the neighborhood since not only the interiors of the apartments but also the exteriors of the apartment buildings were treated to sorely needed renovation and modernization. As a result, I agree with American journalist Adam Sternbergh in *New York Magazine* (2009) who considers gentrification to be a positive factor. Gentrification involves more than the middle-class taking over neighborhoods, and transforming them into IKEA-hoods. It is also about upgrading deteriorating properties and breathing new life into an old part of a city.

Thanks to gentrification, Majorstuen was also privy to a new type of ambience. New tenants moved into premises formerly occupied by small shops that had stood vacant or accommodated stores touting close-out sales. Interestingly, it was not uncommon for them to be converted into cafés. Some are small private companies, like "The Living Room" and "Le Rustique," while others are branches of larger chains, like "The Coffee Brewery," "The Open Bakery" and "United Bakeries."

In other words, Majorstuen has been the site of quite a revolution. The new cafés are far from fashionable. They are ordinary, but not boring. Can Majorstuen's cafés can be described as a new, democratized version of the café?

The role models for these cafés are hardly eighteenth century European cafés. A lot of time has passed since the "premier café" stopped being a trendsetter. Even in the great cities of Europe, the venerable old cafés have either closed down or been transformed into nostalgic museums and tourist attractions.

When the café finally came to Majorstuen, it was a modern variety, which can probably best be described as a hybrid between an American coffee shop and an Italian espresso bar. The contemporary café became an heir of sorts to the temperance café, several of which were located at Majorstuen in the 1920s and 1930s. Their menus featured nonalcoholic beverages, coffee of all continental and the US varieties, juice, smoothies, and light snacks.

Very few of the new cafés have liquor licenses. For example, Café Mistral, the neighborhood café for several of my neighbors in No. 13, might be said to have the Parisian café, albeit a neighborhood Parisian café, as its role model.

It is not hard to determine the source of inspiration for today's cafés. Among the educated middle class, the cinema and TV industries have a huge following. Hollywood and HBO "rule." The members of this class also travel a great deal, and their curiosity about other cultures has turned them into coffee aficionados as well as gourmets. Last, but not least, the educated middle class has developed a taste for the café as a lifestyle.

The Contemporary Café

As this goes to press, it would be no exaggeration to say that there are now as many cafés in Majorstuen as there once were dairy shops, although the cafés are rarely located in former dairy shops, which are generally far too small. Other types of small shops are better suited. In my neighborhood, "Le Rustique" has moved into the premises of a former hardware store. "United Bakeries" is located in a former delicatessen and grocery shop, while the "Coffee Brewery" is in a former florist's shop.

The sheer number of cafés poses formidable challenges for the proprietors. Competition for customers is keen, just as it was in the days of the dairy shops. Like the milk ladies, the café proprietors have to resort to ingenuity and wit, and they have to be more than just a merchant to win faithful, loyal patrons. First and foremost, a café must have a homey atmosphere, preferably with regulars that include celebrities and semi-celebrities. The cafés can also entice customers with discount coupons, freshly squeezed orange juice, or an abundance of the latest newspapers. It is also possible to offer a nice price for the menu selection of the day, for example, a vegetable quiche or a baguette with serrano ham and cheese, and coffee, just the way you want it.

Majorstuen's old bakeries and tea rooms must also be considered a new type of café. They have, in fact, undergone a make-over. Tea rooms with nylon curtains and furniture from the 1960s made of fake leather and steel pipe have been superseded by high bar stools, long tables by the window, and small tables with upholstered chairs. And coffee is no longer simply percolated, bubbling through a filter all day long. Now the menus are definitely of a modern café standard.

In times past, customers were required to order food at the tea rooms. People were only allowed to occupy tables if they ordered something to eat, and the cheapest item on the menu was a sweet bun to go with their coffee. Since the residents of Majorstuen included many widows, a small pot of coffee and a sweet bun was a common order. Such guests could occupy a table for hours. This behavior was tolerated by those who worked in the tea room. However, with the new café concept, a guest can order a light snack if she or he is hungry. The menus feature carrot cake, Sacher Torte, croissants, and sandwiches (which always used to be open-faced in Norway and were called "smørbrød"), although the cost of such fare far exceeds that of the old sweet bun. The new menus and high prices mean that the survivors of the widows in the neighborhood can no longer afford to patronize their old tea rooms. It is very rare indeed to see an old lady in the new cafés without a grandson or a great niece at her table.

Single Households

Thanks to gentrification, Majorstuen has become a far more affluent West End neighborhood than it used to be. The women and men of the educated middle class usually have well-paid positions in the public or private sectors. Many are also single, with no families of their own, either by choice or because of broken relationships, and perhaps they are between relationships. In Oslo and Norway's other urban areas, family and housing patterns have changed dramatically.

While single-person households were rather unusual just two decades ago, today they are common. In fact, they are so common that more than half of Oslo's households are single-person households. The status of the single person has also changed. She or he is no longer the object of pity, or a loser in the struggle to find a partner. As mentioned, this tendency is not peculiar to Norway, an oil-producing nation that is one of the most affluent countries in the world. Family households have maintained their position in all social classes, but single-member households are gaining ground, especially in the cities. It all boils down to the fact that people can afford to live alone.

A few historical statistics about No. 13 might shed some light on the changing family patterns in Oslo's older apartment buildings. The building has the same number of apartments as when it was originally built, that is, eight flats. At the most, No. 13 was home to no fewer than 51 residents. That was in 1928. One single apartment was home to a total of 12 individuals, an old-fashioned extended family with a grandmother and two lodgers. None of households had fewer than three residents, and they usually had five or six. And the households consisted of whole families, with either with small children or adult children. In the late 1930s, the number of residents stabilized at about 38. Some 80 years later, there are only 10 individuals living in the building. Only three of the units are inhabited by two individuals, all middle-aged couples. The apartment that was home to 12 individuals in 1928 is currently occupied by one person whose partner lives elsewhere.

Even back when No. 13 was a relatively densely populated building, the size and composition of a family household could vary. However, it was rare for one person to live alone in a flat for a long time. During the first 30 years of No. 13's history, it was common for families to have a maid, and inasmuch as she only had one evening a week off, she was nearly always in the apartment. The family had their regular meals and routines, and the individual members of the family had to organize their activities accordingly. If someone wanted to be alone, they had to go out. Now, nearly 90 years later, people have to go out to find company and meet their fellow human beings.

Might it be the loneliness of the apartments that furnishes fertile conditions for the contemporary neighborhood café? Inasmuch as the family is devoid of its traditional functions and friends have largely taken over the role of family, the local neighborhood café has become a welcome place. Is it possible that the café may have become the most important third place for those in single-person households? I would venture to say that all modern city-dwellers, single or not, need a third place like a café. You can go there alone because café culture has legitimized loneliness as a positive value equated with quality of life. The café offers a place to meet friends or to sit down among strangers. You can come and go as you wish.

The Remains of the Day

Back to "The Living Room." It is lunchtime and all the seats are taken at the café. Several of the tables are occupied by small groups of young mothers with babies, the fruit of recent years' baby boom at Majorstuen and in the rest of Oslo. Another table is occupied by a young couple, two young men, who only have eyes for each other. The next table over is being used by three coworkers trying to solve a work-related problem. When there are so many people in the café, the solitary café patrons often choose to sit at the high, narrow table in front of the window. They sit almost shoulder to shoulder, but each in their own little world.

By about 2 p.m., most of the lunch guests have left. Tove and Peter have their hands full tidying up, and preparing and garnishing new trays of ciabattas and baguettes. Earlier in the evening, shortly before closing time, business will be very brisk again. People will stop by for coffee on their way home from work, while others will have been there for quite some time, immersed in newspapers.

It's lights out at seven, when the Living Room closes for the evening. The café premises are bathed in a dim light, chairs and stools stacked upside-down on the tables. But at 8 a.m., 13 hours later, a new day will dawn at the Living Room, as old and new patrons take their places at their tables once again. (Translated by Linda Sivesind)

References

Gullestad, M. (1979) *Livet i en gammel bydel (Life in an Old Part of Town)*. Oslo: Universitetsforlaget.

Hjort, D. (ed.) (1996) *Kaféliv. Författare på kafé under hundra år (Café life. One hundred years of writers at cafés), – Vienna/Prague/Budapest/Berlin/Munich*. Avesta: En bok för alla AB.

Høst, I. and Milberg, I. (1916) 1962. *Matlære (Food Science)*. Oslo: Aschehoug.

Londei, J. (2007) *Shutting Up Shop*. Stockport, UK: Dewi Lewis Publishing.

Oldenburg, R. (1999) *The Great Good Place: Cafés, Coffee Shops, Bookstores, Bars, Hair Salons, and Other Hangouts at the Heart of a Community*. New York: Marlowe.

Oldenburg, R. (2001) *Celebrating the Third Place: Inspiring Stories about the "Great Good Places" at the Heart of Our Communities*. New York: Marlowe.

Merriam Webster Dictionary.

Sternbergh, A. (2009) What's wrong with gentrification? *New York Magazine.*
Stenseth, B. (2010) *Nr. 13 – en vestkantfortelling (No. 13 – A West End Story).* Oslo: Aschehoug, Oslo.
Suarez, R. (1991) *The Old Neighborhood.* New York: The Free Press.
Wikipedia.

3

THE THEORY OF THE CAFÉ CENTRAL AND THE PRACTICE OF THE CAFÉ PERIPHERAL: ASPIRATIONAL AND ABJECT INFRASTRUCTURES OF SOCIABILITY ON THE EUROPEAN PERIPHERY

Paul Manning

One of the most celebrated writings on cafés is Alfred Polgar's *Theory of the Café Central* (1926), essentially a feuilleton-manifesto written from within the world of the iconic Viennese literary café. The 'theory' amounts to a somewhat acerbic tongue-in-cheek insider exploration of the characteristically modern forms of stranger sociability and introspective subjectivity bred in this artistic hothouse. Some excerpts:

> The Café Central is indeed a coffeehouse unlike any other coffeehouse. It is instead a worldview and one, to be sure, whose innermost essence is not to observe the world at all...
> If all the anecdotes related about this coffeehouse were ground up, put in a distillation chamber and gassified, a heavy, iridescent gas, faintly smelling of ammonia, would develop: the so-called air of the Café Central. This defines the spiritual climate of this space, a quite special climate in which unfitness for life, and only this one, thrives in full maintenance of its unfitness...

> The Café Central lies on the Viennese latitude at the meridian of loneliness. Its inhabitants are, for the most part, people whose hatred of their fellow human beings is as fierce as their longing for people, who want to be alone but need companionship for it...
>
> But whoever is interested in the Café Central knows all this anyway, and whoever isn't interested in the Café Central we have no interest in...

Why does the *Café Central* need a theory? And what kind of theory would a *Café Peripheral* need? Cafés can express modernity in very different ways, depending on whether the cafés are themselves at home among friends and family in European modernity, or whether they are the vanguard of modernity elsewhere. Prototypical Western European cafés like the Café Central in Vienna or the Café Riche in Paris (Grafe and Bollerey, 2007) instantiate a model kind of café in the metropolitan heart of European modernity (what I am calling generically the "café central"). But cafés located in the European periphery and not the metropole (what I am calling the "café peripheral") cannot help but measure themselves against the prototypical "café central." Such cafés express both aspirations for modernity as well as abjection: the deeply felt absence of the very modernity it sought to express. An incarnation here and now of an urban modernity better instantiated elsewhere, the café peripheral is constantly threatened by its physical situation on the periphery.

There are actually a lot of such "theories of the café central" (Grafe, 2007b), taking "café central" in a wider sense: cafés that happen to occur in places stereotypically thought to be central to self-congratulatory social imaginaries like "European urban modernity." In much postwar social theory, such public places for commensal drinking, what Markman Ellis (2008) calls "architectures of sociability," and what Julia Elyachar calls "infrastructures of phatic labor" (2010), are emblematic of the tenor of interaction characteristic of modern urban public life in general: stranger sociability, a free egalitarian form of association pursued for its own sake without respect to status, interests, or consequences. Following Elyachar, these are places where public *channels* of communication are made visible, they are also places where the imagined others constitutive of modern publics, strangers, anonymous contemporaries, passersby, can be actually seen "face to face, face after face" (Wordsworth, *Prelude*, Book Seven, lines 156–7). Whether these are eighteenth-century English Coffee Houses, nineteenth-century Parisian cafés, or twentieth-century Viennese Cafes, or even contemporary new cafés in postsocialist Russia (Caldwell, 2009) or "maid cafés" in Japan (Galbraith, 2011), such institutions are taken by many social theorists to emblematize and typify some period, some key moment or juncture, of urban modernity (see Ellis (2004) and Laurier and Philo (2007) for overviews of this vast literature). Architectures or infrastructures of sociability like coffeehouses become the laboratories of new modes of sociability and subjectivity, which then become deterritorialized and dematerialized through their homologous propagation in textual circulation. Each such architecture of sociability is directly associated with a specific genre of face-to-face sociability, but they gain special analytical significance by a more attenuated metaphoric association with dematerialized and deterritorialized genres of print circulation: for the English coffeehouse, nothing less than the public conversation of the eighteenth-century Republic of Letters is writ large therein, for the Viennese *Café Central*, the intimate *fin de siècle* Bohemian discourse of the *feuilleton*, for the Futurist cafés of Russia and Georgia, manifestos, and even for Japanese maid cafés, the fictional "2D" world of manga and anime characters who are cosplayed by the maids themselves.

The status of cafés as emblems of urban modernity allows cafés to be ordered with a wide range of other infrastructures (water, electricity, and transportation) that make up the infrastructure networks of modern cities. Such infrastructure networks are not only constitutive of modern urban life *qua* infrastructures, but in the modernist period they become aestheticized, "coming to symbolize the emerging technological 'sublime' of the modern industrial city" (Graham and Marvin, 2001: 45):

> Infrastructure networks, and the complex sociotechnical apparatus that surrounds them, are strongly involved in structuring and delineating the experiences of urban culture and what Raymond Williams termed the "structures of feeling" of modern urban life...Networked technologies of heat, power, water, light, speed and communications are intrinsic to all urban cultures of modernity...Because of this, infrastructure networks are invariably invoked in images, representations and ideologies of urban "progress" and the modern city by all sorts of actors—developers, planners, state officials, regulators, operators, futurists, appliance manufacturers etc...(Graham, 2000: 115)

Julia Elyachar's discussion of "infrastructures of phatic labor," denoting "a social infrastructure of communicative channels that are as essential to economy as roads, bridges, or telephone lines" (Elyachar, 2010: 452) allows us to connect infrastructures of sociability like cafés to these other infrastructural networks that characterize the modernist "structure of feeling" of the city. In particular, she characterizes the Grand Central Coffeehouse of Cairo as a communicative infrastructure, "a place where channels of communication in the public economic space of workshop communities come together and become visible, like train tracks come together in Grand Central Station in New York City" (Elyachar, 2010: 454).

In the classic literature on cafés, then, cafés play a crucial historical role in the formation of *modern sociability and textual circulation*, but in this literature there is little discussion of these architectures of sociability, which serve as a largely presupposed "infrastructure" for these social developments. The literature on such cafés, as Grafe and Bollerey (2007: 02) note, is split between the material (architectural) café, whose design is presented without a human in sight, and the discursive or literary café, in which the only thing that is important about the café are the humans and human sociability and discourse they contain.

Such is the situation of the "café central," a largely theoretical entity found mostly in the centers of European modernity, contrasted with the "café peripheral," the café found in places where infrastructure is problematic, hence always thematic and never presupposed (Star, 1999). The Occidentalist theory of the café central defines European urban modernity by the symptomatic presence of certain characteristic forms of architecture of sociability, but at the same time defines an Orientalist space of backwardness by their absence. The diffusionism of the modernist theory of the "café central" therefore defines the zone of practice for the "café peripheral": To not have these places is to be by turns non-Western, not modern (either peripheral or colonial), not urban, in short, in a state of abjection; to create them in such places is to attempt to reverse these conditions, to express aspirations for a complete progressive transformation of everyday life.

How different do such "architectures of sociability" look when their materiality is foregrounded? The materiality of the café is easily ignored in a largely presupposed European technical modernity in which the infrastructures of sociability are taken for granted, but East European modernism treated the café as a practice directed at the reform of obdurate everyday life, as a way of instantiating an absent modernity in the face of backwardness. In doing so, building or imagining cafés became a way of enacting an aspiration for European modernity, and at the same time pointing up the abject state of the local public infrastructures by their contrast with the backwardness of the streets outside their doors.

To provisionally build such a "theory of the café peripheral," I want to bring together two contemporaneous, but rarely compared, forms of café theory and practice in a country perennially self-conscious of its location on the periphery of European modernity, Georgia (Manning, 2012b). The first kind are what I will call "modernist cafés," including "literary cafés" and their ilk, the cafés imagined and sometimes even built by Georgian modernist intelligentsia. The specific example here will be the café *Kimerioni*, one of many artistic cafés that typified the brief flowering of Tbilisi as an international artistic bohemia (1917–1921) in the wake of Georgian independence and the Russian Revolution and subsequent civil war (Tabatadze, 2011ab). This kind of café will be compared to what I will call "modernizer cafés," cafés like Laghidze's café (on which see Manning (2012a: 118–147)), which also opened in the city of Kutaisi at the turn of the twentieth century and not much later moved to Tbilisi, cafés that concretely express the parallel modernizing aspirations of what would later be called the "technical intelligentsia." Yet these two kinds of cafés represent different aspirations for *different* modernities characteristic of two different Georgian elites living side by side in the same cities: As Harsha Ram (personal communication) elegantly sums up the difference: "if the Kimerioni represents a declassé urbanized intelligentsia that is at once national, metropolitan, and European, Laghidze's café represents a provincial milieu that derives from the impoverished rural gentry from which Georgian national discourse, and Georgian national society, first emerged" (see also Ram, forthcoming).

The Café Kimerioni: a "Chimerical" Café on the Periphery of Europe

> Tbilisi has become a fantastical city. A fantastical city needed a fantastical nook as well, and on one fine day, in the courtyard of No. 12 Rustaveli Avenue, poets and artists opened the "Fantastic Little Inn" (Grigol Robakidze, *Palestra*, cited in Ram (2004: 368)).

To create a café elsewhere, other than in its European metropolitan home, is an ambivalent act. Perhaps a slightly fantastic one. Fantastic because it expresses a modernist aspiration for an absent modernity, a "peripheral modernism" (Ram, 2004), to create a café is an attempt to incarnate an aspirational fantastic "elsewhere" in the here and now, which, once created, can only seem like an intrusion of the fantastic into the everyday world of the periphery.

Georgia's modernists were fairly obsessed with cafés (Tabatadze, 2011ab), not only fantastic cafés but also everyday infrastructures of sociability. Representing both a domain of picturesque ethnographic everyday life as well as a site for the revolutionary change of that everyday life, Georgian modernist artists particularly seem to have been drawn to populating their paintings with architectures of sociability, whether *cafés* in European Paris or *dukanis* (Russian *dukhan*, an originally Arabic word, *dukan*, meaning "store," which is perhaps best translated as "tavern" in Georgian) in Oriental Tbilisi. Their artwork depicting such scenes of commensality in turn reflexively adorned the walls of their favorite *dukanis* and *cafés* (Tabatadze, 2011ab). Like contemporary theorists of the café central, the modernist theory of the café peripheral is an explicitly diffusionist teleological theory of modernity: Europe is the source of modernity, Asia is backward, and Georgia is on the periphery. Correspondingly, modernist representations of the local ecology of architectures of sociability like Zdanevitch's "Old Tbilisi Sketches" (Figure 3.1) implicitly make the European café the apex of an occidental civilizing or modernizing narrative, while Oriental architectures of sociability like the *dukani* belong to an ethnographic picturesque periphery of oriental everyday life that form the raw materials for modernist art or modernization. On the periphery of Zdanevich's sketch, we find oriental *dukanis* and *supras* (feasts), with figures mostly seated on the ground, by contrast, in the center, seated at a table, thoroughly modern boys and girls, and engaged in thoroughly modern forms of sociability and elective intimacy.

There is something strange about the central image: the boy and the girl clearly have been abstracted from *inside* a café so they can be seen synoptically alongside the other figures, which are outside on the street. We know this because the chairs they are seated on are Thonet number 14, this is the classic café bistro chair, the same model we see again in a sketch of Laghidze's café from the same period (Figure 3.2). Zdanevitch has flattened the ecology of architectures of sociability, pouring the contents of the café's interior onto the ground to make it visible alongside the other forms of public sociability that typically happen *outside*, all the while allowing the contrast between European and Oriental modes of sociability to come to light.

Figure 3.1 K. Zdanevich's "Old Tbilisi Sketches" (1) is a typical Georgian modernist treatment of the urban space of Tbilisi by populating it with scenes of ordinary public commensality: (clockwise from the top) a dukan, a stand selling kephyr and "sweet limonat," men seated around a table-cloth (supra) drinking wine, a man and a woman seated on the ground drinking wine in traditional dress, and in the center a boy and girl in more modern clothing seated at a table holding hands. The sketch produces a synopsis of the whole ethnographic range of the ecology of public drinking. (Author Photo).

For many Georgian modernists, it is precisely the absence of the architectures of sociability characteristic of Western modernity, above all the Parisian café, that marks places likes like Kutaisi and Tbilisi as being peripheral, provincial *not (yet) modern, not (yet) urban, not (yet)* European backwaters. For such modernists, the stereotypically exotic and oriental Kutaisi and Tbilisi were typified by the *dukani*, while the stereotypically modern and European Paris was typified by the café. For a Georgian modernist like Grigol Robakidze, the predicament of "Georgian Modernism" (Robakidze 1918) is precisely summed up by the fact that they were forced to make the Kutaisi *dukani* function as a Parisian literary café *manqué*, to utter the names of writers like Baudelaire and Verlaine, drowned out by the din of drunken Georgian song and accordion music.

But as Tabatadze notes in her discussion of the painting of the interior of the Georgian modernist café Kimerioni, the relationship between oriental *dukani* and occidental *café* is much more complex and ambivalent than this simple contrast would suggest: what begins as a contrast can also suggest a synthesis, a hybridization (Tabatadze, 2011a: 65–6, 2011b: 5–6). After all, the modernist paintings that decorated the wall of the café *Kimerioni* include Lado Gudashvili's painting of Tbilisi's *Stepkos Dukani*, an indigenous forerunner of the artistic café, a central figure in the mythology of the indigenous bohemia of old Tbilisi that Georgian modernists were creating at the very same time (for other dimensions of this same mythology, see Ram (2007), Manning and Shatirishvili (2011).[1] The disemia of the dukani thus expresses the ambivalence of peripheral modernists: the dukani is both the oriental opposite of the European café (expressing the sense of exile of peripheral modernists from their true homeland, Paris), and also its indigenous doppelganger (allowing for the production of an indigenous modernist bohemia). Thus, Tabatadze brilliantly argues, by drawing together these two streams of bohemia, the Parisian café and the Tbilisi dukani, the modern and the traditional, the sobriety of café conversation and the drunken excess of the Georgian *supra*, the café Kimerioni is itself a chimerical hybrid, a "café-dukani" (Tabatadze, 2011a: 65–6, 2011: 5–6).

For Georgian modernists, the ecological contrast and continuity between the dukani and the café is an architectural restatement of the burning question of their generation: "Europe or Asia?" But it is more than that, the café is a space for constructing a specific and novel form of everyday life that is opposed both to traditional publics like the oriental dukani *and* to the private spaces of petit-bourgeois domesticity. For Grigol Robakidze, the café is diagnostic of bohemia, it is a house for a bohemian, and bohemia is defined as a category of everyday life (*qopa*), which is the negation of petit-bourgeois everyday life. The everyday life of the bohemian intelligentsia is marked by the café, as opposed to the petit-bourgeois private home or *salon* (Robakidze, 1926).

The Georgian modernist café stands at a double disjuncture, opposed on the X-axis of orientalist social imaginaries to the oriental dukani and on the Y-axis of social hierarchy to the private home or *salon* of the dandy, it defines a form of everyday life opposed to both: an "elsewhere," Bohemia. The term "bohemia" in Georgian modernist discourse is strongly related to the modern Western urban experience, typified by Paris (Gaprindashvili, 1997 [1920], see also Ram (forthcoming)). While the term is strongly associated with a literary demi-monde, and is usually attended by lengthy lists of typical bohemians, aristists, or writers, bohemia is also a product of the urban milieu ("Bohemia, as a typical phenomenon, was created by the city and its history is tied up with that of cities" (Gaprindashvili, 1997 [1920]: 151)), and the "drunken bohemia" of urban cafés produces literature and literary schools such as symbolism and futurism (Gaprindashvili, 1997 [1920]: 153).

Bohemia consists not only of human actors but also of nonhuman ones. While a Georgian modernist description of the fantastic bohemia of Paris, "the homeland and capital city of bohemia" (Gaprindashvili, 1997 [1920]: 155) or the 'fantastic city' of revolutionary Tbilisi (Ram, 2004) will involve an obligatory list of prominent bohemian writers and artists residing there, the fantastic quality of bohemia equally resides in infrastructural aspects of urban modernity: "Paris touches on the fantastic with its preciosity and depravity, its streets and crowds, its tramways, automobiles, carriages, airplanes, noises"' (Gaprindashvili, 1997[1920]: 155). The list includes many of the wondrous, even fantastic, technologies and infrastructures that elsewhere characterize a modern European city for a Georgian modernist like Robakidze, whose similar list in his unfinished novel *Palestra* includes not only emblems of the circulatory city (transport) but also a variety of public infrastructures of sociability like cafés: "the noise of big cities, the multistoried buildings, the endless streets, criss-crossed with mythological webs, countless music-halls, movies, theatres, cafés, stores, rail-roads (above and below ground), tramways, omnibuses, taxis, the ebb, and flow of masses of people."

The aestheticization of urban infrastructures of the modernist technological sublime thus make "the city touch on the fantastic," they become aestheticized, expressive of an "urban fantasmagoria." Hence, Gaprindashvili concludes his list of real infrastructures that contribute to the "fantastic city" by assimilating these infrastructures, and then Paris itself, to the order of fantastic creatures: "Here [there in Paris] appear the most wonderful chimeras. Paris is a true *Kimerioni*." (Gaprindashvili, 1997 [1920]: 155)

It is significant that Paris, a fantastic city full of wonderful chimeras, is dubbed by the same made-up name, *Kimerioni*, which Gaprindashvili's group of Georgian poets gave to their own artistic café (which Robakidze commented was so painted by the Russian painter Sudeikin, that it too appeared to be "full of chimeras") upon its founding in 1919. The name of the café, *Kimerioni*, taken from one of Gaprindashvili's poems, gestures to a fantastic "elsewhere," ambivalently gesturing to the mythological creature the Chimera or the mythological land of Cimmeria (Tabatadze, 2011a: 67 note 124), an fantastic beast or a fantastic place, sets it alongside other such Tbilisian cafés of the same period with fantastic names, *Fantastic Tavern, Argonauts' Boat*.[2]

And in 1919 Tbilisi was indeed a fantastic cosmopolitan "elsewhere" situated on a double periphery to two war-torn metropolitan centres, Russian and European. Tabidze introduces his narrative of the opening of the café Kimerioni with an image of Russian refugee artists and writers, fleeing war-torn Russia for Tbilisi, weeping when they see the warm well-light cafés of Tbilisi, recounting the horrors of war-torn St. Petersburg. On this axis, during the Russian civil war, metropole and periphery were reversed: St. Petersburg had become a dark, frozen city, and Tbilisi, a fantastic fairyland city of electric lights and cafés, "a city that now acquires the attributes of the fantastical formerly ascribed to St. Petersburg" (Ram, 2004: 369).

And yet, how painfully aware are these peripheral modernists that modernity is still better incarnated somewhere further West, a place many had visited before and from which they imagined themselves as exiles: "Our homeland is Paris!" they cried at the opening of *their own* café, the Kimerioni, in 1919, "We should meet up in Paris: it is as if we are sitting in a wagon, dirty and unwashed, we are going to Paris, there is the land of artists..." (Tabidze, 1922: 2). Even in that happy moment, they could not help but see the absence, the lack, an elsewhere, Paris, that could be only imperfectly made present here, in Tbilisi, and the medium of this imperfect transfer is precisely the café. The presence of the café *Kimerioni* here only suggests a brighter world of metropolitan cafés somewhere else. As Harsha Ram (personal communication) notes, in fact Robakidze's claim in his unfinished novel *Palestra* is more radical: that Tbilisi itself, during the brief Menshevik period, briefly became the new centre, displacing both Europe and Russia, Paris and St. Petersburg. The comparison between the West European "café central" and the Georgian "café peripheral" that runs like a leitmotif through that unfinished novel could be taken to imply not abjection or imitation of Europe by Georgia, but in fact supercession.

Laghidze's Café: a European Café on the Periphery of the Oriental Street

In ordinary usage, the term "public" collects together a heterogeneous list of common spaces and infrastructures of the city, including cafés and streets. These spaces are "public" in a rather different sense than the dematerialized common space represented by the public sphere, which cannot be "mapped straightforwardly on to features of the city that are routinely categorized as, and in effect 'collected' by, the idea of public space" (Laurier and Philo, 2007: 266). Charles Taylor summarizes the relation by treating the public sphere as a "meta-space" (a meta-topical space) in relation to these other "topical" public spaces: "But the public sphere, as we have been defining it, is something different. It transcends such topical spaces. We might say that it knits a plurality of spaces into one larger space of nonassembly" (Taylor, 2002: 113–114).

And yet even here, not all "public" spaces are created equal. For thinkers like Habermas, if the polite, sober, reasoned and disembodied conversation of public sphere finds a convenient materialized analog in the idealized sober conversations of the coffeehouse (and not the café, where they serve alcoholic beverages), the disembodied dispassionate reason of the public sphere is even more strongly opposed to the loud, raucous, embodied, coercive politics of the street (see also Manning (2007)):

> The street and the public sphere are therefore fundamentally separate, even opposed, and ideally should be kept apart and devoid of mixing... The street, thus conceived, stands as a semi-metaphoric, almost materialized counterpart to Habermas's public sphere, and the image does present itself of the coffeehouse, notably in its eighteenth-century guise, as the home of a calm public sphere removed from the churning irrationality of the street outside. (Laurier and Philo, 2007: 266)

As Laurier and Philo note, this highly idealized model of the coffeehouse gives the coffeehouse sufficient historical importance to be worthy of study, but at the same time hampers its actual empirical study. In particular, treating the coffeehouse as a place of calm, dispassionate sober reason, securely insulated from the street and its chaotic forms of discourse, ignores the possibility that in the coffeehouses from which the public sphere arose "there may be far more slamming down of mugs, shouting, fisticuffs and more embodied forms of persuasion...and more generally the disruptions and interruptions of the streets and the taverns surely intruded upon the sociospaces of the public sphere" (Laurier and Philo, 2007: 268).

Taken as prototypical examples of their kind, the famous Viennese Café Central and the equally famous Parisian Café Riche (on which see Grafe and Bollerey (2007: 104–117)) are both in some sense extensions of the public space of the street, or rather, the boulevard, but in different ways. What they can both take for granted, however, is a relatively domesticated public exterior. The chaos of the boulevard is, after all, not so very chaotic. The theory of the café peripheral is fueled by aspirations for a modernity embodied in the café central, but the battles waged by the café peripheral are all along its borders, with the sociotechnical obduracy of its urban milieu. Like the Parisian *Café Riche,* the café central is located in a seen-but-unnoticed infrastructural milieu of orderly boulevards and street-lighting, and orderly passerbys, in short, in Paris after Haussmann's reforms (Haine, 1996: 153–159; Graham and Marvin, 2001: 53–7). If the Parisian Café Riche offered a series of transitional spaces between the exterior boulevard and the café interior, with attendant "choice of modes of public presence" (Grafe, 2007a: 23), the Viennese *Café Central* is at first glance a much more securely bounded object, having no shared spaces with the boulevard. But in either case the theory of the café central doesn't need to worry about what is happening just outside in the street, the interesting stuff, forms of sociability and textuality, is all happening inside. By contrast, the interesting part of the architecture of the peripheral café is its spatial, social, and material peripheries, when the action spills outside onto the street, and vice versa.

The birthplace of many of the Georgian modernists discussed above, like Robakidze and Tabidze, was the sleepy provincial West Georgian city of Kutaisi, a beautiful but dying city that Georgian modernists often compared to Bruges (Ram, forthcoming), a city noteworthy not only as being the birthplace of Georgian modernism but also a very different café, Laghidze's café, which represented aspirations for modernity no less than the more famous literary modernists. This café spawned no literary movements and harbored no bohemians, and therefore has no mythic history within the literature of modernism, although, as I have shown elsewhere, it became instead a mythic exemplar of state-directed socialist modernism and the bright future of "cultured consumption" coming into to being under communism (Manning, 2012a: 118–147). In this sense, it represents a shared form of intelligentsia practice, whose goal is the progressive transformation of everyday life, and whose means is the building of cafés.

Even in Laghidze's case, linkages between his world as a member of the "technical intelligentsia" (making soft drinks) and the world of the literary intelligentsia are not hard to find: Laghidze's waters were greeted by fellow Kutaisian writer Akaki Tsereteli upon its opening in 1900 as with a poem celebrating his fruit essences as "the rival of drinks—of wine, of beer, of water, and of milk" (Sigua, 1980: 9); in the socialist period the Russian poet Evgenii Evtushenko famously compared the "secret" of Laghidze's waters with the "sorcery" of Tabidze's poems, thus aligning the seemingly incommensurable worlds of material and verbal production of these fellow Kutaisians (Sigua, 1980: 4). According to their shared progressive framework, civilization, or if you prefer, modernity, was something located not merely in the future temporally, but also spatially to the West, in Europe. Like many of Kutaisi modernists, Laghidze journeyed to France with an eye to seeing their cafés, and though the literary modernists saw in these cafés an emblem of a fantastic bohemia, and Laghidze saw in them better ways to make and serve soft drinks, both saw in Parisian cafés emblems of an aspirational modernity, and saw in building cafés in Kutaisi or Tbilisi a way of overcoming the abjection of the periphery.

If the café Kimerioni in Tbilisi was "fantastic," Laghidze's waters in Kutaisi was no less so. The Laghidze's waters café and factory became emblematic of Georgian modernity because it opened in the capital of the West Georgian province of Imereti, Kutaisi, at the dawn of the twentieth century, and also because it was like all that is perceived to be modern: novel and atypical of its place and time. And this was also its problem, because its dissonant relations to its own urban context are constantly thematized. In its early years, virtually all of what we hear about this café in the newspapers are things happening on its precarious peripheries. Here I touch on just three elements that represented a certain modernizing impulse, the aspirational aspects of the café: First, that the café was lit by electric lights, secondly, that it sold cold soft drinks (cooled by ice made by the same private electric power plant); and third, its precarious location on a central boulevard of Kutaisi. What I show in each case is how each of these aspirational moments also illuminated the abjection of the relation of the café to the broader ecology of public spaces and infrastructures.

In Tabidze's striking image, Russian émigrés fleeing the October revolution and civil war in Russia wept and kissed the earth when they saw the electric lights of the cafés in Tbilisi. By 1919, cafés with electric lighting were already taken for granted aspects of the urban cityscape, like the rest of the order of public infrastructures, noticeable only in its absence (Star, 1999). But a significant part of the modernity of the café is its close association with the modern "fairyland" aesthetic effects associated with electric lighting, part of the "technological sublime" mentioned earlier: For example, Robakidze's novel *Palestra*, which is essentially a theory of the café and urban modernity turned into a novel, has many of these elements in its description of his fantasy of a prototypical European café sitting on the side of an enormous boulevard of a European city: "From afar the café appears like the reddish-yellow eyes of Isis... The café dazzled with soft white electric lights. The main color of the café was orange"; "The café WIEN was lit up in in electric light. The electric light thawed in the color of lemon rind." As McQuire (2004) notes, "even from the first, electric illumination exceeded a purely functional role," electrical lighting was as often initially as much a matter of public spectacle as public utility helping produce "the formation of a distinctively modern sense of space."

The clearest single way that Laghidze's café represented European modernity was that Laghidze's café was the first establishment in Kutaisi, and probably much of Georgia, that had electric lighting. One imagines a spectacle in which there is a single brilliantly lit café beside a park in the midst of an otherwise dark city lit by the dim glow of household lanterns and candlelight. Laghidze thus not only transformed public space but also created night-life in Kutaisi. However, this very same private commercial electric lighting casts shadows, the corresponding absence of any public "police" lighting (Schivelbusch, 1995: 142–3), so the very existence of the electric lights of this café illustrates the general failure of state-led modernization. At the same time, because the fuel supplies of the electric plant depend precariously on other aspects of state-infrastructure like the railroad, the night life of Kutaisi that depends on the Laghidze Café is in turn dependent on the unreliable public infrastructure of the railways. One writer, commenting on how Kutaisi had emptied out that summer (as Georgian cities often do, as people return to their ancestral villages), complained that even Laghidze's was empty, as an index of just how barren the cityscape became in the summer. In case of Laghidze's factory, this writer added, the reason was that because of a railroad closure, there was no fuel oil to produce electricity for the electric lamps, or, had there been electricity, "if there had been even a single butterfly left in Kutaisi," that's where they would have been (*Tsnobis Purtseli* b 2242: p.2 August 21, 1903).

The revolutionary private production of public lighting was actually a by-product of the need to produce ice to cool the actual product of the café: soft drinks ("artificial mineral waters" (Manning, 2012a: 101–2)). While the café of social theory hardly ever have anything on the menu other than "modernity," drinks matter to actual cafés, the fact that Laghidze sold cold nonalcoholic beverages into the night is, in the Georgian context of primarily masculine alcohol-fueled sociability, *revolutionary*. It was in this context that Georgian poet Akaki Tsereteli celebrated Laghidze's as the "rival of other drinks," most of which drinks were alcoholic ones, wine and beer. Not everyone shared an equal enthusiasm. According to a local correspondent, already by 1903, Laghidze's artificial waters

> have been embraced strongly by both men and women, mostly by women, however. Drinking waters has become the fashion [*moda*]: whether you want to or not, still you consider yourself obliged to buy at least one bottle of waters, even if you don't drink even one glass of it. Even though money is spent pointlessly, but it can't be helped. Still a man can cool his heart with cold waters. (*Tsnobis Purceli* 2198: page 3, July 3, 1903)

The fact that Laghidze's café served such nonalcoholic drinks allowed it to be an almost unique locale in which men and women could engage in sociability in public, a predominantly fashion which, according to this commentator, men suffered as an unavoidable obligation. However, as this commentator then notes, the "rivalry" between Laghidze's waters and beer does not end there:

> Only beer has become a nuisance: often men who have gotten drunk at a feast visit the factory and stubbornly demand beer. Then they start swearing and cursing with obscene words and sometimes they even picks fights, by which means they cause a great annoyance to society. The police however are nowhere to be found, to pack these young hooligans off from there, where it is necessary. At the very same time, five or six policemen guard the police station, you would think the whole treasury was stored there... (*Tsnobis Purceli* 2198: page 3, July 3, 1903)

Laghidze's linked together a specifically feminine form of cultured public comportment and fashion (*moda*), identified with genteel aristocratic "society," which was opposed, specifically, to the rather plebeian masculine behavior of public drunkenness and beer consumption, which was in turn associated with the perennial problem of hooliganism, and incidentally exposed the failure of the state (the police) to pacify the public spaces of the street.

If the example of electric lighting shows the café spilling into the street (illustrating the failure of the state to provide public lighting) then here we find the hooliganism of the street spilling into the café (again, illustrating the failure of the state to provide police). This brings us to my last example. Laghidze's café, prominently located on Kutaisi's large central boulevard (Sigua, 1980: 9.n2), is like the Parisian cafés on which it is modeled in that it is continuous with the public space of the street. While a customer in a Parisian café poised at the edge of one of Haussmann's boulevards might experience the passing traffic as a purely visual panorama, a sort of seated flaneurie, no different in principle from the way a passenger in a railway car experiences the passing landscape, the cartoon "Kutaisi entertainment" suggests that the central problem of a similar café in Kutaisi is the much greater sensory traffic between the street and the café.

But I want to talk here only about the spatial aspect of the assemblage. While the Viennese café is ordered with other forms of architectural interior, such as the private home, which makes it possible to categorically oppose this public space of sociability to private spaces of sociability, the Parisian café in particular is actually part of a set of urban reforms that attach it to a new form of street, the boulevard.

But the café is part of a spatial assemblage with the boulevard, and indeed, the architecture of the café is typically liminal half-inside and half-outside, resembling other architectures that fascinated modernists like the balcony and the courtyard of traditional urban architecture (Manning, 2009). Certainly Laghidze's café mirrors architectural tendency, located along one of Kutaisi's new boulevards across from the park. The problem is that this exposed situation on the porous boundary of the central boulevard that allows it to typify in a satirical cartoon the more general problems of "Kutaisi entertainment" (Figure 3.2), in which the problematic underachievement of normative European modernity was writ large.

The central problem of "Kutaisi entertainment" is that the backwardness of village life intrudes on the genteel urban public life of the city, as a villager carrying what appears to a tank full of sewage in a primitive cart is leaking this malodorous waste in

Figure 3.2 "Kutaisi entertainment" (1903).[3]

front of a local café, whose sign reads (in Russian) "Laghidze's Mineral Waters," whose residents decorously ignore the intruder while holding or wearing kerchiefs to their faces. The cartoon, one of many by the same artist on the theme of public infrastructures (Figure 3.3), reminding us with Elyachar that cafés *are* part of the order of infrastructures, draws attention to the infrastructural gulf between the aspirations for "European" modernity (represented locally by Laghidze's café) and the fact that throughout this period Kutaisi, unlike Paris, lacked any kind of sewer system or other provisions for urban sanitation. But the Laghidze's café in Kutaisi is not, after all, the Parisian Café it seeks to be, any more than a Kutaisi *dukani* is. Indeed, according to the ideology of the times, to make it so would require nothing short of a transformation of all aspects of public urban life, a standardization and segregation of things like genteel entertainment and sanitation, orderly city and disorderly village, Europe and Asia.

Figure 3.3 "The last days of Tbilisi's 'Konka' Tramway" (1904).[4]

Notes

1. For this and other artwork decorating the walls of the Kimerioni, the entry on "Tbilisi Artistic Cafes" at http://www.modernism.ge/.
2. For the artwork of Sudeikin in the Kimerioni and the "Land of the Argonauts" see the entry on "Tbilisi Artistic Cafes" at http://www.modernism.ge/.
3. Tsnobis Purtseli 1903 No. 2238 Suratebiani Damateba 143 page 4.
4. Tsnobis Purtseli 1904 No. 2523 Suratebiani Damateba 277 page 4.

References

Bollerey, F. (2007) Setting the Stage for Modernity: the Cosmos of the Coffee House. In Grafe, C. and Bollerey, F. (Eds) *Cafés and Bars: The Architecture of Public Display*. Oxford: Routledge, pp. 44–81.

Caldwell, M. (2009) Tempest in a Coffee Pot: Brewing Incivility in Russia's Public Sphere. In Melissa, C. (Ed.) *Food and Everyday Life in the Postsocialist World*. Bloomington: Indian University Press, pp. 101–129.

Ellis, M. (2002) The Devil's Ordinary. Electronic Document. http://www.cabinetmagazine.org/issues/8/coffeehouse.php, accessed October 10, 2010.
Ellis, M. (2004) *The Coffee House: A Cultural History.* London: Weidenfeld & Nicolson.
Ellis, M. (2008) Introduction to the coffee house: a discursive model. *Language & Communication,* 28, 156–164.
Elyachar, J. (2010) Phatic labor, infrastructure, and the question of empowerment in Cairo. *American Ethnologist,* 37(3), 452–464.
Galbraith, P. (2011) Maid in Japan: an ethnographic account of alternate intimacy. *Intersections: Gender and Sexuality in Asia and the Pacific* Issue 25, http://intersections.anu.edu.au/issue25/galbraith.htm.
Gaprindashvili (1997[1920]). Bogema [Bohemia]. In Orjonikidze, I. (Ed.) 1997. *Evropa tu Asia?* [Europe or Asia?]. Tbilisi: Literaturis Matiane, pp. 151–156.
Grafe, C. (2007a) The Architecture of Cafes, Coffee Houses and Public Bars. In Grafe, C. and Bollerey, F. (Eds) *Cafes and Bars: The Architecture of Public Display.* Oxford: Routledge, pp. 6–43.
Grafe, C. (2007b) Scenes from the Café—Gossip, Politics and the Creation of Personalities: A Selection of Texts from and on Cafes. In Grafe, C. and Bollerey, F. (Eds) *Cafes and Bars: The Architecture of Public Display.* Oxford: Routledge, pp. 82–93.
Grafe, C. and Bollerey, F. (2007) *Cafes and Bars: The Architecture of Public Display.* Oxford: Routledge.
Graham, S. (2000) Introduction: cities and infrastructure networks. *International Journal of Urban and Regional Research,* 24.1, 114–119.
Graham, S. and Marvin, (2001) *Splintering Urbanism: Networked Infrastructures, Technological Mobilities and the Urban Condition.* London: Routledge.
Haine, W. S. (1996) *The World of the Paris Cafe: Sociability among the French Working Class, 1789–1914.* Baltimore, MD and London: Johns Hopkins University Press.
Laurier, E and Philo, C. (2007) A Parcel of Muddling Muckworms': Revisiting Habermas and the English Coffee-houses. *Social & Cultural Geography,* 8.2, 259–281.
Manning, P. (2007) Rose-colored glasses? Color revolutions and cartoon chaos in postsocialist georgia. *Cultural Anthropology,* 22.2, 171–213.
Manning, P. (2009) The City of Balconies: Elite Politics and the Changing Semiotics of the Post-socialist Cityscape. In Van Assche, K., Salukvadze, J., and Shavishvili, N. (Eds) *City Culture and City*

Planning in Tbilisi. Where Europe and Asia Meet, Lewiston, New York: Mellen Press, 71–102.

Manning, P. (2012a) *The Semiotics of Drink and Drinking.* London: Continuum Press.

Manning, P. (2012b) *Strangers in a Strange Land.* Boston: Academic Studies Press.

Manning, P. and Shatirishvili, Z. (2011) The Exoticism and Eroticism of the City: The 'Kinto' and his City. In Darieva, T., Kaschuba, W., and Krebs, M. (Eds) *Urban Spaces after Socialism: Ethnographies of Public Places in Eurasian Cities.* Frankfurt: Campus Verlag, pp. 261–281.

McQuire, S. (2004) Dream Cities: The Uncanny Powers of Electric Light. *Scan,* 1(2) http://scan.net.au/scan/journal/display.php?journal_id=31.

Polgar, A. (1926) Theorie des 'Cafe Central.' In Polgar, A. (Ed) *Kleine Schriften.* Vol. 4. pp. 254–59. English Translation in Grafe and Bollerey (2007) 91–93.

Ram, H. (2004) Modernism on the periphery: literary life in postrevolutionary Tbilisi. *Kritika: Explorations in Russian and Eurasian History,* 5(2), 367–382.

Ram, H. (2007) The sonnet and the mukhambazi: genre wars on the edges of the Russian empire. *PMLA* 122. 5, 1548–1570.

Ram, H. (Forthcoming) *Crossroads Modernity. Aesthetic Modernism and the Russian-Georgian Encounter.*

Robakidze, G. (1918) Gruzinskii modernism. *ARS. Ezhemesiachnik iskusstva i literatury,* 1, 51.

Robakidze, G. (1926) Kote Marjanishvili. *Duruzhi,* 1, 2.

Robakidze, G. *Palestra.* Unpublished Manuscript.

Schivelbusch, W. (1995) *Disenchanted Night: The Industrialization of Light in the Nineteenth Century.* Berkeley: University of California Press.

Sigua, G. (1980) *Mitropane Laghidze.* Tbilisi.

Star, S. L. (1999) The ethnography of infrastructure. *American Behavioral Scientist,* 43(3), 377–391.

Tabatadze, T. (201a) *Artistuli Kape Kimerioni da misi Mokhatuloba. T'pilisi, 1919 Tseli* [*The Artistic Café* Kimerioni *and its Wall Painting. Tiflis 1919.* Tbilisi: Tbilisis Apolon Kutatelidzis Sakhelobis Sakhelmtsipo Samkhatro Akademia.

Tabatadze, T. (2011b). "The Artistic Cafe *Kimerioni* and its Wall-painting. Tiflis, 1919. [English summary of Tabatadze (2011a). http://www.modernism.ge/index.php?action=page&p_id=364&lang=eng.

Tabidze, T. (1922) Kimerioni. *Barikadi,* 1–2. 87.

Taylor, C. (2002) Modern social imaginaries. *Public Culture,* 14.1, 91–124.

4

Cafés, Third Places, and the Enabling Sector of Civil Society

Graham Scambler

Cafés have never been mere buildings within which proprietors and staff take money in exchange for refreshments. Bricks and mortar might contain them, provide their parameters as it were, but the concepts they conjure up and the needs and aspirations they satisfy reflect the praxis of time and place and the idiosyncrasies of individual taste and quirkiness. For writers, artists, and would-be revolutionaries, the concept is likely to call to mind the Viennese salons in the years straddling the beginnings of the twentieth century, or the smoky liaisons and workplaces of "engaged" freelance philosophers like Camus, Sartre, and de Beauvoir in *Les Deux Maggots* in mid-century Paris; for many a refugee places of respite, familiarity, and recognition; for builders and truckers, an "all-day English breakfast" and a kick-start to long physical and fatiguing shifts. There are historical and sociological narratives of emergence and the flourishing of institutions and markets, and mundane person-by-person storytelling. This chapter is a sociologically oriented contribution to a burgeoning literature on what is sometimes termed psychogeography.

Setting the Scene

Neither coffee nor cafés are novel phenomena, although their biographies have distinct origins. Coffee was entirely unknown before the middle of the fifteenth century, when it was absorbed initially into the drinking habits of people in the Red Sea basis, infiltrating the Ottoman Empire in the sixteenth century. It was in the course of the sixteenth century too that it came to Britain. The first English coffeehouse opened in Oxford in 1650; two years later an Armenian or Greek migrant from Smyrna, Pasqua Rosee, financed by his merchant employer Daniel Edwards, set up an establishment in St Michael's Alley at Cornhill (Luttinger and Dicum, 2006). The habit of coffee drinking and the emergence of the coffeehouse have fascinated Western historians ever since, not least because of their associations with the eking out of a civil society beyond monarchical reach. The period from the end of the seventeenth century through the "long" eighteenth century witnessed a momentous change. In the words of Cowan (2005: 2),

> the crucial social legitimacy for both the coffee commodity and the coffeehouse was provided by the unique combination of a genteel "culture of curiosity" and a rapidly growing commercial world centred in London. Civil society in early modern Britain developed as a product of this mixture of gentlemanly curiosity and urban commerce. The viruosi provided the catalyst that spurred the initial commercial interest in coffee and the development of the coffeehouse as a significant social institution, but this initial interest was then seized upon and transformed by the exigencies of urban sociality.

It was Habermas (1989) who most comprehensively theorized the significance of the coffeehouse for civil society and the public sphere, in England rather than Britain and in London in particular. For him the coffeehouse epitomized the *public use of reason* within the norms and confines of the day. It was of course not without its limitations: it was open to "all comers," *excepting women*; it was a commercial and urban venue, hence it was *bourgeois*; but it was nevertheless a place in which sober rational debates might and did occur on all maters, including politics, from a platform of equal participation. Coffeehouses, in short, exemplified what has been called the *enabling sector* of civil society: that is, a popular meeting place where public argument and agitation might have its genesis, occasionally peaking to spill over into the *protest sector* of civil society to take more organized forms in pursuit of effective influence in the public sphere of the lifeworld (Scambler and Kelleher, 2006). Habermas' seemingly romantic and "Whiggish" characterization of the coffeehouse has been criticized but not refuted; several attempts to falsify the core claims of his "Habilitation" thesis have unravelled in the process.

Habermas sees little residue of the eighteenth century coffeehouse in contemporary cafés, in London or elsewhere. Formal democracy may have been anchored in twentieth century notions of citizenship and institutionalized, but this progressive shift has neither underwritten the public use of reason nor led to capitalist or political elites being held to proper account. The measures bullied through by the post-2010 Cameron-led coalition of "Con-Dems" in Britain bears eloquent testimony to this, inciting protests, even "riots." Formal "parliamentary" democracy is no substitute for substantive democracy. Instead coffeehouses have become, at best, "third places," a term coined by Oldenburg (1997) to denote community foci, places where people routinely gather to catch-up, talk, and exchange views as well as gossip. But Oldenburg too is downbeat: he sees cafés, bars, local stores, and "hangouts" in the USA occupying a declining role in an increasingly impoverished civil society (see his chapter).

Of course patriarchal, *bourgeois* coffeehouses were never the sole option for coffee drinkers in London. Moreover the present-day city bears little resemblance to its predecessor in the seventeenth and eighteenth centuries. Nor have the distributions of its personnel and their resources, material and symbolic, remained static. London has grown almost beyond recognition. This is not the place for a detailed chronology or sociology of demographic, structural, institutional, or cultural change, but a contextualizing comment or two are in order and relevant to the discussion that follows.

London Pre-Starbucks

At the beginning of the seventeenth century, London's population was around 200,000. By 1700, it had increased threefold and was vying with Paris as the largest city in Europe. A hundred years later, during the twilight of the period of the European Enlightenment that so intrigued Habermas, a period to which the English maybe contributed more than has conventionally been credited to them (Porter, 2000), the population of London, now Europe's premier city, was approaching a million and was on the cusp of further and far more rapid expansion. If in 1800 one in 10 people in England and Wales lived in the metropolis, by 1900 it had reached one in five. By 1900 over four million individuals dwelt within the boundary of what came to be called "inner" London, and over six and a half million in "outer" or "greater" London. The other English boom towns of the industrial revolution had not been able to compete (although paradoxically London itself never became an industrial city): "London," Porter (1994: 207) writes, "thus formed a classic example of what has been labelled the 'primate city', one disproportionately vaster than all the others in the kingdom, a city relating not just to the nation but to the world." The peak figure for the population of greater London exceeded eight and a half million in 1939, after which there was a decline until the 1990s. The total currently is around seven and a half million.

The longstanding rivalry between coffee and tea took off soon after Rosee welcomed his first clients in London's Cornhill in 1652. By the start of the nineteenth century, tea had been usurped and displaced by coffee, succeeding even ale as the national drink. At the same time, the coffeehouse underwent a protracted period of class-based retrenchment, from which it only reemerged—as coffee prices fell—with the sponsorship of Arab, Turk, Greek, Sicilian, and other émigrés in the course of the second half of the nineteenth century. London's Soho, a magnet for émigrés, proved a key location. Although there were perhaps as many as 1,400 coffeehouses in the London area by the end of the nineteenth century, they had not regained their earlier influence; moreover the *bourgeois* coffeehouses had largely given way to the more lowly coffee room (Brandon, 2007).

The twentieth century saw an inauspicious start for coffeehouses, but following the success of milk bars from the 1930s, the coffee bar, seen initially as something of a "low-life" resource, proved extremely popular in the 1950s. In 1945, Gaggia adapted the espresso machine to create a high-pressure extraction that produced a thick level of crema; and by 1946 the *cappuccino*—christened for its resemblance to the color of the robes of the capuchin monks—had been delivered: the unique selling point of the classic café had arrived. Coffee bars were rife in London's Soho by the mid-1950s, the first, a classic Formica café called *The Mocha* at 29 Frith Street, being opened by Gina Lollabrigida in 1953. Rippling rapidly out from Soho, these cafés became magnets for political activists, jazz players, *nouveau* existentialists, and beatnik baby boomers, anticipating and feeding the cultural explosion of the 1960s.

The 1970s witnessed a rise in unemployment as oil prices rocketed and Britain's manufacturing base halved, signalling a recession that left only a handful of diehard café groups untroubled: the Lyons' Wimpy Bars (established in 1954) and the Golden Eggs (set up by Reggie Kaye and others in the early 1960s). This proved to be a significant juncture, a transition from Fordist, industrial, welfare statist or organized capitalism to post-Fordist, postindustrial, postwelfare statist or reorganized capitalism, from first to second modernity. By the onset of the Thatcherite 1980s cafés were struggling, further challenged by a revitalized pub culture, burger conglomerates, and a mushrooming of sandwich bars. Meanwhile things were stirring in the USA and a "speciality coffee industry" was beginning to flex its commercial muscle. In the new consumerist landscape, American cafés encouraged people "to hang out, to idle away the afternoon, and to do so without paying very much" (Luttinger & Dicum, 2006: 159).

London: the Starbucks Era

Starbucks was founded in 1971, but after Howard Schultz came to the helm in 1987 it came to promise more than cheap idleness. Graduating from selling roast beans to selling coffee, its marketing mission rapidly crystallized:

> Americans are so hungry for a community that some of our customers began gathering in our stores, making appointments with friends, holding meetings, striking up conversations with other regulars. Once we understood the powerful need for a Third Place, we were able to respond by building larger stores, with more seating. In some stores we hire a jazz band to play on weekend nights...People don't just drop by to pick up a half-pound of decaf on their way to the supermarket, as we first anticipated. They come for the atmosphere and the camaraderie. The generation of people in their twenties (now in their thirties) figured this out before the sociologists. As teenagers, they had no safe place to hang out except shopping-malls. Now that they are older, some find that bars are too noisy and raucous and threatening for companionship. So they hang out in cafes and coffee bars. The music is quiet enough to allow conversation. The places are well-lit. No one is carded, and no one is drunk (Schultz and Yang, 1997: 120–121).

Sharper than sociologists Schultz may have been, more entrepreneurial he certainly was; his aspiration to provide new third places was marketed as an attempt to realize Oldenburg's vision.

Starbucks became a major corporation, its senior executives decamped from concerns like Nike, Burger King, McDonalds, and 7-Eleven. With in excess of 10,000 outlets worldwide, it enjoyed partnerships with the likes of PepsiCo, Anheuser-Busch, United Airlines, Marriott, Hewlett-Packard, and Barnes and Noble. In the process, arguably, it became "the antithesis of the independent speciality coffeehouse, providing a corporatized, homogenized retail experience with a consistent but not outstanding product" (Luttinger and Dicum, 2006: 162). Schultz's aim to extend the artisanal gourmet coffee ethic hit obstacles. Starbucks has become part and parcel of Ritzer's (1996) *McDonaldization* of society, a process now far from exclusive either to America or indeed the Occident. This evolving pragmatism has spawned the

Pumpkin-Spice Latte, the Mint Mocha Chip Frappuccino, and the Strawberries and Crème Frappuccino Blended Crème. Starbucks' espressos and lattes are not Italian; they are as American as Coca-Cola. And when Ray Charles' posthumous *Genius Loves Company* went triple-platunum in 2004, a quarter of the sales were from Starbucks' outlets.

Starbucks has been heavily condemned too for out-muscling local independent rivals, making them offers they can't refuse, denuding neighborhoods of their historic charm and uniqueness. This muscle-flexing and readiness to fight has arguably been most destructive in Europe and in cities like London. In 1998, Starbucks acquired the London-based but American-founded and owned Seattle Coffee Company for $83 million, thus spearheading an assault in London, the United Kingdom, and throughout Europe. The explicit goal was to match the global ubiquity of McDonalds. Since the mid-1990s it has in fact been castigated for its promulgation of multiple evils through its usurpation of the otherwise inoffensive coffee bean (Box 4.1) (see also Wright (2004)).

Box 4.1 "THE BUZZING WOULD NOT GO AWAY..."

"The buzzing would not go away. Without opening my eyes, I hit the clock radio. My brain managed to hold one coherent thought: caffeine.

I staggered into the kitchen to brew a cup of coffee. It took 100 beans—about one-sixtieth of the beans that grew on the coffee tree that year. The tree was on a small mountain farm in the Antioquia region of Columbia... Farmworkers wearing shorts, T-shirts, and sloshing backpacks sprayed my tree with several doses of pesticides synthesized in Germany's Rhine Rover Valley.

Workers earning less than a dollar a day picked my coffee berries by hand and fed them into a diesel-powered crusher, which removed the beans from the pulpy berries then encased them. The pulp was dumped in the Cauca River. The beans, dried under the sun, travelled to New Orleans on a ship in a 132-pound bag. For each pound of beans, about two pounds

> of pulp had been dumped into the river...At New Orleans, the beans were roasted for 13 minutes at 400 degrees F. The roaster burned natural gas pumped from the ground in Texas. The beans were packaged in four-layer bags constructed of polyethylene, nylon, aluminium, and polyester. They were trucked to a Seattle warehouse in an 18-wheeler, which got six miles per gallon of diesel. A smaller truck took the roasted beans to my neighborhood store. Two hours after I finished my morning cup, my body had metabolized the coffee. Most of the water and some of the nutrients passed into the Seattle sewer system.
>
> I drink two cups a day. At that rate, I'll down 34 gallons of Java this year, made from 18 pounds of beans. The Columbian farms have 12 coffee trees growing to support my personal addiction. Farmers will apply 11 pounds of fertilizers and a few ounces of pesticides to the trees this year. And Columbia's rivers will swell with 43 pounds of coffee pulp stripped from my beans."
>
> (Ryan and Durning, 1997: 184)

In the first decade of the twenty-first century, Starbuck hit harder times, giving Wall Street palpitations in the process. Dairy prices rose, the United States experienced a downturn even before the global financial crash of 2008–2009, and there was a cut-price caffeine onslaught from the likes of McDonalds and Dunkin' Donuts. Starbucks' shares fell by 42 percent during 2007. Maybe, commentators speculated, one Starbucks every 0.07 square miles in New York, was enough; in New York and elsewhere, it seemed, "Starbucks saturation" might have been reached. But this slow-down found little echo initially in Britain. At the time of writing Starbucks has 20,366 stores worldwide (13,123 in the USA). It has been experimenting recently with "unbranding" via the expedient of promoting "local coffee houses," automated systems and diversification (Clark, 2008).

One unintended consequence of Starbucks' commercial aspirations was a spate of genuine attempts to more closely ape Habermas' depiction of the eighteenth century coffeehouse, or, more modestly, Oldenburg's third place, for example. in the celebrated "Socrates Café," or the general cultivation of public spaces for deliberation (see *conversationcafe.org*). However, its lucrative coffee branding also heralded the arrival of a light, fluid, postmodern, or consumer society, perhaps best captured in the writings of Bauman (2007). And the consumer society is most appositely analyzed in terms of the ongoing "colonization of the lifeworld" via the commodification *even of the public use of reason* (Scambler, 2002). Capitalism's endpoint, Wallerstein (1998) reminds us, is the "commodification of everything." The same Starbucks café, it will be maintained, can simultaneously hold prospects for money's subversion of the rights encapsulated in citizenship and for an enabling sector of civil society.

It is revealing to report in this context that in October 2012 a Reuters investigation uncovered systematic tax avoidance by Starbucks in the United Kingdom. The company paid just £8.6 million in corporation tax over 14 years, despite generating £3 billion in sales it paid no tax at all in the three years prior to 2012, despite sales of £1.3 billion. Starbucks offered to pay £20 million in back tax, but this has not satisfied its critics. So in the months leading up to the publication of this discussion, courtesy of the actions of UKUncut and other activist bodies, *Starbucks has featured in the protest as well as the enabling* sector *of civil society.*

The Contemporary Café as a Material and Social Space

The present always resonates with and contains the past and future. The old survives in the new and the new comprises anticipated projects. This is true alike of material and social space. So organized capitalism or first modernity can be discerned in the physical and psychosocial properties of today's London cafés, as can, to the prophetic eye, missions as yet unarticulated let alone accomplished. In this section, a provisional typology of London café locales is proffered, in the next a companion typology of café usage. There may well prove to be statistical associations between the two. "Greasy spoons," offering filling, no-nonsense, all-day English breakfasts as a prelude to stamina-sapping physical shifts, rarely host students completing coursework assignments, and many a Starbucks offers more to the later than the former. But associations like this are contingent and admit of many exceptions. The typologies here consist of Weberian ideal types. Ideal types are analytic constructs: in other words, they are not amalgams of actually existing examples, but rather purposive, second-order characterizations pertinent to the sociological matter under discussion.

(1) Material Spaces

Nine types of café are identified in Box 4.2:

> Box 4.2
>
> - The *transport café* (or *caff*) in London and other urban locales may have had its heyday in the 1950s but it endures, coffee increasingly rivalling tea as the drink of choice; nor is instant coffee as predominant as it was. The *caff* is a daytime social institution, opening and closing early, its prices modest, catering for the transient, the manual working-classes and what has been called their "displaced segment," a more precise term than "underclass" (Scambler and Higgs, 1999). It is a paradigmatic stopping-off point.
> - The *independent café* is intent on survival: resisting the brands of Starbucks and its protégés, it has become a brand that challenges branding. This is a tradition defying the fabricated rebranding of the traditional. Heir to the provincial tea shop, it is archetypically a family concern, dependent on a mix of long-term regulars and customers either nostalgic for a receding past or uncomfortable with the present and the hypercommercial, consumerist future they see unfolding. Contemporary economic orthodoxy fears for the independent café.
> - The *specialist café* offers excellence. Excellence here implies an authentic, positive, defiant project, a head-up challenge to back personal taste. These stand-alone cafés are often seen by their customers as modern oases in the desert of the postmodern. Noted for their ambience, they are redolent of

modernity's staid, elitist "high" culture in an era of dynamic hybridity and branded difference.
- The *incidental café* comprises bars, hotels, and restaurants and accents space rather than place. Coffee is an afterthought, an extra, a secondary and generally cheap option tagged onto an individual's primary activity: to eat, consume alcohol, or spend the night. It is coffee drinking in a place which is a nonplace, having no properties exclusive to or characteristic of coffee consumption.
- The *store café*, often franchised, offers brief respite to those indulging in the archetypical postmodern practice of shopping. In this contemporary sense, shopping, especially in those islands of aspirational consumerism, malls, is less a functional necessity than a chasing of dreams and fantasies. Aspirational consumerism, promiscuous consort of a rhetoric of choice, can be seen sociologically as embedded in a class-motivated culture-ideology of consumption (Scambler, 2007).
- The *bookstore café*, also typically a franchise, is a store café with a difference: it caters predominantly to the declining minority who read, browse, and, sometimes, purchase books. In some respects, it is a third place or public forum in waiting. The ethos readily found in the USA, permitting students of all ages to carry piles of reading matter to consult over a coffee or three, alone or in dialog with their peers, regardless of the risk of spillage and despoilment, is gradually being accommodated in London and other of Europe's university cities.
- The *internet café* epitomizes the postmodern world of instant global communication. These "network nodes" offer seating and a coffee and access to the technologies of talk and chatter, a prepaid chance to check emails, polish a powerpoint presentation, consult a contractor, send a kiss, and reassure parents that everything is okay even if the money is running out. It is a place of virtual dealings and relationships.
- The *travellers' café* caters for people who have been apprenticed to need transit stops and transit pick-me-ups or diversions, caffeine in a polystyrene beaker, whether at Heathrow destined for the USA or Wimbledon en route to Dorking; or indeed waiting for a bus to anywhere. Coffee here fills a gap: it is a prop, an adult's comfort blanket, something to do while nothing needs doing.

> - The *chain café* is epitomized by Starbucks, since imitated by a score of ambitious offspring. All the brands are here, as is the facility to confess to – and commodify – sins committed. Charges and critiques challenge less-extant practices than the business capacity to rebrand these practices. Every coffee bean seems destined to retain its innocence, sown, nurtured, processed, set before the coffee lover with an irresistible mix of altruism and compassion (but see Wright, 2004).

There is of course movement between these categories. Moreover, Starbucks has "seen off" many an independent, store, bookstore, and travellers' café. But, the contention here runs, there is an amalgam of place and space in this typology, a material substratum, which informs and buttresses the much more pertinent business of café usage to which I now turn.

(2) Social Spaces

There exists no one-to-one correspondence between the material and social spaces comprising cafés. Bestselling treatises, creative dialog, and sharp deals can reach their conclusions in *caffs* or store cafés, and job interludes or moments of rest from bodily fatigue enjoyed in the domains of the incidental or bookstore café. It is in this spirit that the typology of café usage is ventured (Box 4.3):

> Box 4.3
>
> - The person who visits a café to *observe*, *le flaneur*, is an elusive, composite, semiheroic character, a bequest from Baudelaire and Benjamin's musings on the emergence of nineteenth century Paris as a modern city. He, and it was a "he," was most at home among the elegant Parisian arcades, on the very cusp of their displacement by "a more strictly regimented topography" (Coverley, 2006: 20). He symbolized the rise of the modern amidst the debris of the old, a nostalgic figure personally bound up with the passing of the familiar. He was the embodiment of the dynamic city, the "patron saint of

cultural studies" (Solnit, 2001: 199). In London at the start of the twenty-first century, it is more difficult to distinguish between *le flaneur* and one of his, or now her, successors, the "stationary traveller." Duc Jean Floressas des Esseintes in Huysmans' *A Rebours* affords a role model. Walking the streets is rejected in favor of "mental travel": his *flaneury* is thoroughly domesticated, an exercise of the imagination from the comfort of an armchair. This transmutation of *le flaneur* provides a benchmark for café usage. In twenty-firstst century guise, he or she remains the wry, semidetached observer of city life and personnel, but now the café stool, chair, even armchair, provide the observation point.

- *Le flaneur* is not relaxed, cannot but observe. Those who visit cafés to *relax*, to take a deep breath and the weight of their feet, to recoup, only observe fortuitously. Their intent is an honest and straightforward one: they are en route, making an incidental and frequently unplanned stop to refuel, pausing in malls at shoppers' rests, purchasing fried breakfasts between jobs at *caffs*, or, more literally, calling in at chains at motorway stops while driving from A to B, reaching B being the overriding objective.
- Increasingly in cities like London cafés are places to *deal*, to do business, sites where colleagues can agree agendas and allocate tasks or where fresh deals can be struck. Good or bad news can be conveyed over a tall cappuccino. The territory tends to appear to neural, defusing relations that might otherwise be fraught. "Marks" can more easily be "cooled out" in cafés.
- People also visit cafés to *socialize*. Sociability can be pursued for its own sake or for its potential to oil wheels or deliver outcomes unrelated, or even antagonistic, to work. The gathering of people who are like-minded or have interests in common is another types of café usage. London has witnessed a spread of coffeehouses to cater for specific religious or ethnic groups, affording a bounded sociability (Clayton, 2003). It is this category of usage too that best fits Oldenburg's notion of third places or, more ambitiously, a would-be enabling sector of civil society. It is a form of usage of political import: acorns in the enabling sector occasionally give rise to oaks in the protest sector. Clayton (2003) prophecies renewed vigour and influence for cafés as third places in the twenty-first century London.

- Cafés can also provide a refuge, a solitary and secluded corner in which to bury oneself, a means to *escape*. In this case usage is nonsocial and defensive, carrying none of the offensive third place potential for organizing or resisting change. The café is a place of escape, offering a barrier between a hassled self and a transitory or generically hostile or threatening social world.
- Returning to a café to *get a fix* implies more than a passing need for caffeine, solitude or seclusion. It is the addiction of *l'habitue*. The will has surrendered to a routine. Replete with props—local newspaper, weekly magazine, puzzle book—the drinker subsides with a practised sigh of relief. It is usage characterized by ritual: visits occur at the same time every day, with the same greeting, seat occupied and drink ordered. In this familiarity of the neat and predictable is loneliness accommodated and, maybe, what Giddens (1990) calls "ontological insecurity" held at bay. It invokes what has elsewhere been called a "familiarity bond" (Scambler and Tjora, 2012).
- Going to a café to *work* can be a deliberately solitary activity, if associated with a project-oriented, positive rather than negative mind-set. Writers are prime examples, and almost any café can suffice; specific books or articles may even be associated with particular material spaces, even tables. Sometimes what appeals is working, cut-off by a steady act of will, against a background of hustle and hubbub. These words were drafted next to a table of lunching women, a lively knitting circle swapping stories in Foyles' bookstore café in Charing Cross Road.
- This same café on Foyles' first floor hosts jazz events, the last one I attended marking the publication of Julie Blackburn's biography of Billie Holliday (Blackburn, 2005). So another usage is to *entertain*. Others cafés too win their clienteles by offering entertainment, typically of a predictable genre. Talks, debates, poetry readings, and music of every caste and description have homes in cafés. Each attracts its connoisseurs and devotees.
- Last but not least come the thirsty and hungry, those who simply seek replenishment via a cappuccino, bacon, and egg sandwich or bag of salted peanuts or crisps. The need here is corporeal not mental: the function is to *refuel* the better to press on with the tasks that lie ahead.

It bears repetition that (1) there is no easy correspondence between the material and social spaces that comprise London's contemporary cafés; and that (2) individuals—with the possible exception of *l'habitue*—can and do make multiple uses of cafés: the switch from socializing to observing and back again can occur almost instantaneously. Rewritten as a matrix, the material and social ideal types outlined here (9 × 9) identify 81 cells. Few of these have been subject to study, perhaps surprisingly given the vigorous American chain-led resurgence of public coffee consumption toward the end of the twentieth century. These are ubiquitous material spaces of daily salience to growing numbers of London's citizenry; but they have precipitated neither a microsociology of social encounters or sociability nor a macrosociology of the café as a possible third place successor to the old politicized English coffeehouse. It is macrosociology that provides the focus in the paragraphs that follows.

Café Futures: "De-colonizing" the Lifeworld?

The point has been tacitly made that London's heterogeneous café users are not simply chain-and brand-led "postmodernized" consumers. It is a moot point, however, just how much of what has survived of the *modern citizen* through to the post-1970s era of reorganized or financial capitalism or second modernity. Is there any echo of yesterday's masculine and *bourgeois* but nonetheless politically oriented public sphere in today's cafés? While none of the 81 cells of the matrix are necessarily empty, a few warrant special attention and suggest psychogeographical hypotheses of relevance to this question.

Before the politics of decolonization is broached directly, however, it is important to consider certain unintended consequences of the reemergence of the café as a positive and maybe functional site of sociability. Cafés, first, remain sites of old-style, face-to-face networking of the kind that enthused the interactionist sociology of the Chicago School and Goffman in the 1950s and 1960s. They have more than a little of the classic lifeworld-oriented third place about them, where people meet and talk, especially on a regular basis, bonds of shared interests and concerns emerge. Cafés are among the new loci of what have elsewhere been referred to as "familiarity bonds" (Scambler and Tjora, 2012), sites where people might find distraction, peace, a sense of belonging, or at least shelter under the umbrella of protectiveness afforded by diffuse and variant forms of social capital (Giddens, 1990).

Like any third place, however, cafés also carry potential as sites for the enabling sector of civil society, and it is this possibility that is addressed in the remaining paragraphs. One change levelled by Negt and Kluge (1993) and Thompson (1995) against Habermas' (1989) original analysis of the eighteenth century English coffeehouse is that alternate non-*bourgeois* sites go missing. By focusing on the contemporary café, is this not to reproduce Habermas' initial class-bias? Five propositions are relevant here:

1. effective non-*bourgeois* solidarity is still likely to be class based (see below);
2. the short-term prospects for working-class consciousness leading to effective collective action for political change have receded since the 1970s, as the *invisible* "class politics of the advantaged" has for the time being—in circumstances favorable to it—seen off any "class politics of the disadvantaged" (Scambler and Scambler, 2012);
3. it is 'new social movements' that Habermas and others understandably see as the most promising avenues of resistance to the status quo, and these in combination represent what has been called a "culture of challenge" (Scambler & Kelleher, 2006);
4. new social movement activity might yet trigger class-based activity;
5. the café (in the enabling sector) is an as yet underinvestigated site of (middle-class *and* working-class) political opposition (in the protest sector).

As far as corporate and political *elites* are concerned, with the exception of a specialist café or two, it is to the exclusive clubs and discrete restaurants of London's West End or to private households that they adjourn to do business. Moreover, it is difficult to foresee a reprise to John Dryden's role as fulcrum of public debate at Will's Coffee House in seventeenth century Covent Garden, counting the likes of Samuel Pepys and Alexander Pope among his avid listeners (Brandon, 2007) (celebrity dinner parties for play-wrights in Hampstead are a poor substitute). It is the cell phone and *virtual* communication that establish rationale and framework for many an elite and oppositional *actual* encounter today. It is a mark of the degree of the systemic colonization of the public sphere of the lifeworld that so little place-based actual public debate and dissension is generated around the fissures and edges of elite culture.

Doubtless this has in part to do with the emergence of what Oborne (2007) perspicaciously identifies as a post-modern "political class." Members of this "class" are mostly career politicians, committed and highly focused aspirants set on a well charted if still slippery trajectory to the power bloc at the epicentre of the apparatus of the state. Party politicians and part machines have become brazen exponents of strategic action. During New Labour's time in office, from 1997 to 2010, Peter Mandelson, Machiavellian guru to Blair, was as indebted to the Americans in this respect as are London's latest café chains. He, together with the likes of Alistair Campbell, aping James Carville's service to Bill Clinton, remain symbols of the strategic, clandestine interpenetration of political and media elites in Britain. This unholy alliance unravelled somewhat as the Murdoch empire imploded courtesy of the *News of the World* hacking scandal and the resultant Leveson Inquiry; it remains a crisis of consequence for Cameron and his acolytes within the post-2010 "Con-Dem" coalition government. Party political and governmental politics since 1997 afford incontrovertible evidence for Habermas' thesis of the general decline in opportunities for the public use of reason.

What journalists like Oborne often gloss over, however, are social structures, which are less easy to grasp and translate into lay currency than events. Oborne's national political class has become more not less answerable to compact, compelling and increasingly global or transnational financial and business interests; and these interests are class based. Oborne's political class has become more controlling or "regulatory" even as its subservience to these interests has grown; and in the process it has become less accountable to its electorate (Moran, 2003). In Habermasian terms again, the gap between the "formal" democracy of parliamentary process and "substantive" or participatory democracy has been revealed afresh. If social class has increased its *objective* salience for people's circumstances, however, it has undoubtedly lost much of its *subjective* salience for identity-formation; hence the enhanced role and potential of new social movements. In the short term at least, new social movements appear to hold out as much or more promise as agents of social change than do (working-) class-based solidarities. Oppositional consciousness is likely to be conceived at a remove from extant elites, and maybe, via conversations, arguments, compromises, shared interests, and ad hoc and local campaigning, serendipitously, amidst the proliferation of outlets of our "café society."

It is against this background that a case for research into the use of cafés, in particular independent, bookstore, network node, and chain cafés, to socialize (in *actual* face-to-face interaction) and to work (in *virtual* liaisons) might be advanced. This is the café not only as third place but also, just possibly, as an enabling sector of civil society in waiting. So these 10 cells of the 81-cell matrix might repay further investigation as material and social spaces with some prospect of hosting what Habermas (1984; 1987) terms lifeworld rationalization or decolonization. In short, they are candidate sites for holding to account Oborne's political class and, more circuitously, *but more urgently*, the financial and business interests that set the parameters for its agenda: class-driven commodification is prior here, state bureaucratization derivative (Scambler, 2002).

Since the "Arab Spring" of 2010, the contagious, transnational spread of politically motivated "occupations" (mostly targeting corporate greed), and the rapid growth of protest activity in London and elsewhere directed at multiple facets of the austerity program of the "Con-Dem" coalition government, all material and symbolic bases of oppositional resistance need to be covered. This encompasses the role of cafés in today's networked society. There are of course many other theses emanating from the new café society worthy of examination, but for which there is insufficient space here. What has become of *flaneury* in London at the start of the twenty-first century? What of the café as *l'habitue's* home-from-home? How significant is the café as a postmodern imaginary? How does time routinely spent over a regular *cappuccino* bear on day-to-day quality of life? Some of these questions receive attention in other chapters of this book. As far as this chapter is concerned, however, I hope a prima facie case has been made for the empirical investigation of the contemporary café, and of café society, as a possible third place site of lifeworld resistance to systemic colonization against the background of growing inequality and public disaffection (Scambler and Scambler, 2012).

References

Bauman, Z. (2007) *Consuming Life*. Cambridge: Polity Press.
Blackburn, J. (2005) *With Billie*. London: Jonathon Cape.
Brandon, D. (2007) *Life in a 17th century Coffee Shop*. Stroud: Gloucestershire.
Clark, A. (2008) Wall St gets palpitations over caffeine fuelled growth. *The Guardian*, Monday 7 January.
Clayton, A. (2003) *London's Coffee Houses: A Stimulating Story*. London: Histporial Publications.
Coverley, M. (2006) *Psychogeography*. Harpenden: Merlin.
Cowan, B. (2005) *The Social Life of Coffee: the Emergence of the British Coffeehouse*. New Haven: Yale University Press.
Giddens, A. (1990) *Consequences of Modernity*. Cambridge: Polity Press.
Habermas, J. (1989) *The Structural Transformation of the Public Sphere: An Enquiry into a Category of Bourgeois Society*. Cambridge: Polity Press.
Luttinger, N. and Dicum, G. (2006) *The Coffee Book: Anatomy of an Industry from Crop to the Last Drop*. New York: The New Press.
Moran, M. (2003) *The British Regulatory State: High Modernism and Hyper-innovation*. Oxford: Oxford University Press.

Negt, O. and Kluge, A. (1993) *The Public Sphere and Experience.* Minneapolis: University of Minnesoa Press.
Oldenburg, R. (1997) *The Great Good Place: Cafes, Shops, Community Centres, Beauty Parlours, General Stores, Bars, Hangouts and How They Get You Through the Day.* New York: Marlowe & Co.
Oborne, C. (2007) *The Triumph of the Political Class.* London: Simon & Schuster.
Porter, R. (1994) *London: A Social History.* London: Hamish Hamilton.
Porter, R. (2000) *Enlightenment: Britain and the Creation of the Modern World.* London: Penguin.
Ritzer, G. (1996) *The McDonaldization of Society.* Thousand Oaks, California: Pine Forge Press.
Ryan, J. and Durning, A. (1997) *Stuff: the Street Lives of Everyday Things.* Deattler: Northwest Environmental Watch.
Scambler, G. (2002) *Health and Social Change: A Critical Theory.* Buckingham: Open University Press.
Scambler, G. (2007) Social structure and the production, reproduction and durability of health inequalities. *Social Theory and Health*, 5, 297–315.
Scambler, G. and Higgs, P. (1999) Stratification, class and health: class relations and health inequalities in high modernity. *Sociology*, 32, 275–291.
Scambler, G. and Kelleher, D. (2006) New social and health movements: issues of representation and change. *Critical Public Health*, 16, 1–13.
Scambler, G. and Scambler, A. (2012) Underlying the riots: the invisible politics of class. *Sociological Research Online*, http://www.socresonline.org.uk/16/4/25.html.
Scambler, G. and Tjora, A. (2012) 'Familiarity bonds': a neglected mechanism for middle-range theories of health and longevity? *Medical Sociology Online.*
Schultz, H. and Yang, D. (1997) *Pour Your Heart into It: How Starbucks Built a Company One Cup at a Time.* New York: Nyperion.
Solnit, R. (2001) *Wanderlust: A History of Walking.* London: Verso.
Thompson, J. (1995) *The Media and Modernity: A Social Theory of the Media.* Cambridge: Polity Press.
Wallerstein, E. (1998) *Utopistics, Or, Historical Choices of the Twenty-First Centiury.* New York: The New Press.
Wright, C. (2004) Consuming lives, consuming landscapes: interpreting advertisements for Cafedirect coffees. *Journal of International Development*, 16, 665–680.

5

THE CAFÉ COMMUNITY

Ida Marie Henriksen, Tomas Moe Skjølsvold, and Ingeborg Grønning

I am sitting in one of the popular cafés in town. I have been sitting here the last 4 hours, observing how people are moving. It is a windy, rainy October day. Outside the big windows I can see how people are rushing by, shivering. The atmosphere inside the café is peaceful with lit candles and jazz streaming out of the speakers. At arrival in the café I noticed that the tables and chairs outside are accompanied by heaters, pillows and blankets. Torches and welcoming signs on the outside invite passing guests to stop by.

A few years ago, the three authors of this text were gathered in what can be described as a quite typical urban café in Trondheim, one of the largest towns in Norway. There was nothing conspicuous about the incident, we were having coffee, doing some work, discussing the weather, music, various TV-shows, and solving the problems of world politics, more or less at the same time. Around us everyone else seemed to be doing the same. This is café-life as we know it: people coming and going, ordering drinks, eating food, talking, reading, writing, kissing, and feeding babies. Observed from a distance the café can appear as an autonomous organism; a gooey flow of bodies operating in structured patterns, together constituting "the café."

One peculiarity about the three who met at the café at this exact day is that we were there as social scientists joined together by a curiosity about the nature of this "goo," How exactly is it that the café comes to be? If we zoom in and place the café-organism under a social-scientific microscope, what types of practices, habits, patterns, similarities, differences, or other oddities are we likely to find? In short, what is it that people "do" when they visit cafés? Further, how can the practices and habits of café guests inform us about "what" the café is as a social space? In other words, what are the functions of a café in the everyday lives of ordinary café guests?

The notion of "community" is central to our discussion. Is it in any way fruitful to talk about "the café" as a community, and if so—how? The question of community concerns at least two related aspects of the café-experience. First is the empirical question of whether or not different "types" of café guests be identified through the study of actual café routines. Second is the more theoretical question of social potential, in other words how the qualities of a community like that of a café could play a role in other desired social processes such as integration, democratization, gender equality etc.

These kinds of theoretical considerations about the café have been discussed at length in the past. For Habermas (1989), the coffeehouses of the eighteenth century represented an ideal public sphere, a place where men (but only men) could gather to discuss political ideas regardless of social status, and thus come to new and better understandings about the world. While this view can be criticized as utopic and naïve, modern thinkers also highlight that there is a significant social potential in the café as a space. Ray Oldenburg (1999), for example, highlights that cafés can become so-called "third places" and that third places are distinct from first or second places; homes and workplaces. Third places share a range of characteristics that feeds into creative social potential. They represent a sort of "neutral ground" in the sense that no one is obligated or tied down in the place. Further, they function as "levelers," which means that the social or economic status of individuals outside the third place do not matter on the inside. While many activities can take place in the third place, conversation is often the main activity. Third places are also characterized as accessible and accommodating, and they harbor "regulars"—a group of people who provide some stability, or a certain "tone" to the social quality of the space. Further, third places are characterized by a low profile, a "playful mood" and those who occupy them often report that they have warm feelings of possession or belonging to the third place; it is a "home away from home." Oldenburg's ideas are echoed in Delanty (2003), who refer to cafés as "in-between spaces," increasingly important in the everyday lives of people.

For us, the idea that cafés can serve as third places or in-between spaces first and foremost serve as inspiration for empirical scrutiny. From Oldenburg's account, it is quite clear that simply calling a building a café does not make it a "third place." Rather, it becomes a third place due to certain combinations of built space, café guest behavior, and experience. The habits of café guests, their routines, and café-practices are highly important to the establishment of a third place or any other sense of community. In this chapter, we are interested in these practices and the routines of café guests and what these practices mean to those who carry them out.

Research Methods

Through a five-year period starting in 2007, our group periodically interviewed with café customers. We also did systematic observations of life in the café, focusing on behavior and interaction between café guests. A total of 70 interviews and 32 written observations were conducted in 14 cafés located in Trondheim and Oslo.

Observational notes were written on laptops or note books while the interviews were recorded digitally with informed consent from the interviewees. Both interviews and observations were later transcribed and analyzed using an inductive strategy, generating "empircally close codes" (Tjora, 2012) through HyperRESEARCH.

The Multiplicity of Café Guests

Through our ethnographic work at a number of cafés, we have observed a range of different ways to take part in café life. This suggests that the café can serve different purposes and that its significance as a social space might vary considerable from one café guest to another. In what follows, we consider different ways of using the café space, through ethnographic explorations of a set of ideal-typical café guests.

The Takeaway Customer

At its most instrumental, the café serves as place to get a caffeine-fix. Interpreted in this way, the takeaway customer is perhaps the most obvious junkie. But is there more to the café for the takeaway customer?

Our observations suggest that takeaway customers typically dominate the café space in the mornings. This is not so strange of course; it suggests that the quick stop-over for coffee might be part of a morning routine—on the way to work, heading for school or after delivering children in the kindergarten. These customers typically do not occupy the café for long. They queue and leave. One of our interviewees explained, "I do not sit down in a café very often, but I often stop" by. In other words, dropping by for a coffee can become part of a routinized pattern of behavior, a practice that does not only provide a dose of caffeine but a sense of stability. Our observational data supports such an assertion. Most takeaway customers are highly "competent" as café guests. They know what they want, how to queue, and what to expect from other guests and staff. One of our interviewees explained how changing jobs resulted in altered morning routines. One of the things he missed the most was the daily stop-over for takeaway coffee at his favorite café: "It was tough; it took some time to get used to." This had to do with the coffee, of course, and also with the sense of recognition and repeated social interaction, which was granted after just a few visits. Repetition of the same routine quickly leads to gaining a status as a "regular," a status that implies mutual recognition between staff and customers. One way that this can be manifested is when the barista simply starts making "the usual" just by the sight of the regular. Thus, even for takeaway customers who simply stop by for a few minutes, the café experience can be more than a simple cup of coffee. It might serve to situate the morning routine in a broader social setting, and in turn their presence in the café as takeaway customers in a distinct way adds to the shaping of the café as a "third place" through adding to the general buzz and hum that characterizes and separates one café from another or a café from any other "third place."

The Regulars

While takeaway customers can become regulars, this is of course not always the case. Regulars are a quite diverse group. We remember that Oldenburg (1999) described the regulars as vital to third places, in the sense that they provide stability, a certain tone and a particular "feel" to the place in question. The following is an excerpt from our observational notes in one of the cafés we studied:

> It is around noon. An elderly couple enters. They sit down to the left of the entrance, at the innermost table. She orders a cup of coffee, he drinks a pint. Before sitting down they had collected a stack of newspapers from a newspaper-rack located next to the entrance. Opposite of the couple, in another section of the café I observe a single man, dressed in clothes that suggests he was young in the 1970s. He reads the newspaper while drinking a coffee. The three perform the exact same act; they drink, read and from time to time gaze into the air.

We don't know for certain that the observed guests are regulars, but their behavior correlates well with how regulars describe what they do. These guests feel comfortable; they feel at home, they know where they want to sit, what they want to do, and how to relate to facilities like a newspaper-rack. In one conversation with an interviewee, the following could be heard:

> Do you ever go to other cafés downtown?
> No. I mean, I stop by here every morning before I go to town [...] Yes, I mostly come here for a coffee and the newspaper.
> Do you meet people you know here?
> Well, the staff. We chat.

Another example of regulars knowing the physical facilities was found when we observed two teen girls who were working on their laptops. Their laptops were connected to what appeared to be the only power outlet in the café, which they confirmed. Thus, being a regular implies some sort of competence and mastery of the physical space in combination with a feeling of being "at home."

So what else makes these guests "regulars"? They frequently visit the café, of course, and they know their way around the place, but there is more. The status as regulars is established in interaction with the staff and is deeply tied to a sense of mutual recognition. The regular feels acknowledged as a person who belongs in the café, as a natural inhabitant in this home away from home. One interviewee referred to this as the "cheers-effect," a place where he was recognized. The regulars feel comfortable with the staff and other café guests. One interviewee explained it in the following way:

> So, when you go to this place, do you recognise those who work there?
> Yes. After a while it becomes very pleasant. You say hello and greet them and have a friendly chat. I mean, I don't know their names, but you sort of know them anyway. And they know the regulars [...] You might even meet them on the street, and then we nod and greet each other.

The relationship between regulars and staff is maintained through routines like ordering the same coffee every day or small talk. Through informal interviews with baristas across town, we have learned that regulars are highly appreciated guests. However, just like the regulars do not know the name of the staff, the staff do not know the names of the regulars. Instead, regulars are often given nicknames like *"trippel latte," "Big latte without foam,"* and *"shake-the-coffee-pot-man"* are all examples. The names were often related to the practices and habits of the customers who had become regulars. Sometimes such habits could be so routinized that the barista would just begin making "the usual" as soon as they see the face of a regular. A café employee described a usual situation:

> The cheese cake and coffee-gang would come every Saturday and make the same order. As soon as we saw them, we would just begin making the cheese cake and coffee.

This type of friendly gesture was performed as a special treat to regulars, making them feel welcome, appreciated and "taken care of." This illustrates that the staff actively takes part in shaping and maintaining the role of regulars.

As we have seen, being a regular can imply a range of things. Takeaway customers, individuals, couples, and groups can all become regulars. They become regulars through frequent visits to the café, competence and know-how of the particular café, and in interaction with the staff. In this way, they are essential in establishing the café as a community, and are probably vital in establishing some sort of identity for the café in question.

The Café Worker

Many café guests use the café as an office. With their laptops open, typing away on word documents or excel worksheets, these guests illustrates the fluidity both of what work is in our age, and of what the café is. A third place is not a work place or a home, but it is an in-between space. But it can easily be used for work purposes. Some cafés might facilitate this for instance through offering free Wi-Fi. One of our interviewees explained that he used the café as a temporary office: "I'm just making a quick stop to check a few things online before I get on the bus to the airport."

Of course, we do not know that everyone who appears to be working is actually working. As Hampton and Gupta (2008) have suggested, some café guests appears to work, while they actually surf the web or do other leisure-oriented activities. These guests are referred to as "placemakers." They occupy the place with their laptops as a center of attention, but they remain open and "engageable," which means that placemakers are prone to boost the social potential of a café. On the other hand, "true mobiles" the use café as a creative space for productivity and work, but are typically less likely to engage in unplanned social interaction (cf. chapter 8 for more details). Meeting colleagues for lunch is another way of using the café as a workspace:

> The atmosphere is alright and you get a decent cup of coffee. People relax more in a café than in a meeting room. It's easier to talk amongst other people, as long as it's not confidential stuff.

While some people use the café to meet colleagues for lunch or have meetings, others prefer working alone with their laptops. However, they are not the only ones that visits the café by themselves. The "loners" will be described in the following section.

The Loners

Many visit cafés alone on a regular basis. Interestingly, however, a large group of our interviewees described this practice as unthinkable. Hampton and Gupta have suggested that this type of "public solitude" is often actively pursued by placemakers. As Erling Dokk Holm (2010: 144) has pointed out, this type of solitude does not necessarily imply loneliness. Rather, for those who seek public solitude, the café offers an invisible community. One way to describe such communities is as a sort of communication community (Delanty, 2003), based on new forms of belonging. Such an abstract sense of belonging can be anchored in a multitude of potential personal traits such as religion, gender, or lifestyle. These identities and senses of belonging are manifested in unstable, open, and individualized groups and are often organized as invisible communities without a fixed common point of reference.

Cafés often have "profiles" reflecting certain attitudes or tastes. In some cases, they might even be seen as reflecting or promoting certain types of lifestyles. This can accentuate a feeling of belonging. One of our interviewees ascribed the sense of belonging to the music played in his favorite café:

> The music is important. In both my regular cafés the employees play good music. It's important for them to play good music. I don't know if they have the customers in mind when they choose the music, but it attracts us and makes us want to come back.

One interviewee explained that he visited cafés in solitude every day: "For me it's a sanctuary. I get away from the social world and can relax, read a book or just breathe." This fascinating quote also points to the ambiguity of a concept such as public solitude. This respondent, in his quest to escape the problematic aspects of "the social world," precisely set out to visit a social space like the café. For others, the café is much more clearly a link to the social world, an escape from the loneliness of the home, into the public solitude of the café. The following is an excerpt with an interview with a mother who was on maternity leave from her work. During this period she visited cafés alone by herself on a regular basis.

> *Interviewer*: So what do you do when you are alone in the café?
> *Mother*: I read the newspaper, budget the family economy, and plan the day. Drink coffee and watch people.
> *Interviewer*: Why don't you just do these things at home?
> *Mother*: I do these things at home as well. But I have become this kind of person that like to see other people. To see others have a soothing effect on me.

Others describe how the social qualities of the café space provide discipline for the time spent in solitude. The respondent in the following interview had trouble concentrating on reading if he was alone at home, but the public solitude of the café helped him focus:

> I read books, which is the reason I go to the café. I try to read a book a week, and this is my motivation for coming to the café. I can't do it if I'm not sitting in a café in solitude, I can't find the time.

The public solitude of the café can provide the needed discipline to pursue such projects, and it also leaves the café guest more or less open to unexpected social interactions. While our observations and interviews clearly suggest that there is a vast social potential in visiting the café alone, other simply can't stand the idea. This brings us to our next category of café guests.

The Social Guest

People pursuing public solitude seek a quite subtle form of community. We have labeled our next category of café guests as "the social guest" because of their preference for direct and planned social interaction in the café space. Consider the following excerpt from one of our interviews:

> *Interviewer*: Do you ever go to a café alone?
> *Guest*: No, that never happens. I don't need to. I prefer my own living room [to be alone]. When I go to cafés, I do so to be social, not to be social by myself.

In other words, the café serves a quite different purpose for these guests. While loners for various reasons seek the community of public solitude, the social guests use it as an arena to maintain social ties that are not necessarily related to the café. Typically, the social café guests use the café as a place for interaction with their close ones. The following two descriptions from an observational session during weekday lunch hours can serve as examples:

> A man comes in to the cafe, and a lady who is sitting down at a corner table stands up. "Hey!" she exclaims and they embrace each other. She says "I almost started to worry about you." The man replies, explaining that his delay was due to an appointment with a doctor. The woman offers to buy him some food, but he explains that he cannot eat. However, he would like to have some coffee.
>
> Two long haired men sit in a café booth eating burgers [...] They discuss the music in the room. One of them utters with a distinct dialect: "That's Dylan". They continue to talk about music, before they take on their jackets and leave the café.

The social guests often explained how the café served as a natural hub for whatever social engagement they were planning. It provides the infrastructure for sharing a meal or a quick coffee, but more importantly it serves as a space where social interaction over a period of time feels natural. In this way, the café is different from the supermarket, the library, or other public spaces—its main attraction is precisely "the social." One student interviewee explained: "We want to hang out and do stuff together. Since we don't have the world's greatest fantasy we usually end up meeting in a café."

So far all our observations have concerned adults. However, particularly during the weekends it is also possible to observe many children in cafés with their families. Like this observation illustrate:

> Two young boys and a lady who is most likely their mother enters the café. The boys are shouting out what they want to eat. When they reach the second floor where I am seated, I change my mind about the lady; she is most likely their grandmother.

As a social space, the café provides a room for social interaction across generations, in this case probably facilitating quality time for grandmother and grandchildren. Another of our interviewees explained how he used the café as a substitute for his living room, and that he frequently brought his daughter there to have a cup of hot chocolate and play a game of chess.

The observations and quotes above illustrate how social guests use cafés in various ways to maintain friendships and family relationships. Social guests feel at home in the café, they are quite comfortably able to establish a private zone of comfort in this space. This point became especially clear when we observed a peculiar kind of social guests: those who seek the café to explore their mutual romantic feelings. The following is a typical example:

> A formally dressed couple in their thirties is having an intense conversation. They walk over to the counter, order and find a seat by the window. They place their coats and bags on the

surrounding chairs. They kiss and touch each other, all while discussing something. They are eating a plate of salad, while her hands are placed on his thigh the whole time. She spills some topping on her hand and he quickly kisses it away. She replies with a kiss on his neck. They laugh and look into each other's eyes. After a while they put on their coats and leave the café, holding hands.

In other words, some café guests are happily able to engage in quite intense romantic behavior in the café. In summary, we have seen that the café space invites a multitude of social interaction: everything between friendly conversations, games of chess, and intense romance is tolerable. Perhaps this is part of the cafés attraction as a third place: it opens up for both planned and unexpected sociality in many forms. This quite naturally brings us to the next group of café guests we have identified, a group that completely dominates certain cafés at certain times a day: the mothers.

The Mothers

In a number of our sessions of observation we could observe large groups of mothers with babies and prams. In Norway, it is quite common for public health centers to organize social groups of mothers with newborn babies. Normally these mothers do not know each other before they become part of these groups. Once organized, the group will typically meet in a café or somewhere else about once a week. This observation serves as an illustration:

> Four mothers with prams enter the café. The one in front points at the coach where I am sitting. They start discussing where to sit and end up combining two tables in the middle of the café. They place the prams around the table. Two mothers picks up their babies. One brings her baby with her while moving towards the counter. The other mom cuddles with her pink dressed baby while the rest of the mothers discuss how much their babies are sleeping.
> A lady sits alone with her baby on a sofa, rocking her baby back and forth. Across the table there are three other mothers

with babies on their laps. Two of them are drinking tea and the last drinks a cafe latte. Meanwhile at the counter queue, two other women are talking. They extend their necks every time they hear a baby crying, probably because two prams near the sofa belongs to them.

For many "new" moms, the café seems to serve as an extremely important social arena. Becoming a mother is in many ways quite disruptive: it is a plunge into a new stage of life, a phase where many seek new social contacts. Our observations and interviews suggest that the cafés may facilitate this. This is perhaps the most direct observation of the social potential of cafés that we have in our material. The mothers come to the café first and foremost as mothers, regardless of what other roles or social positions might have in their daily lives. In this way, the café seem to serve as a leveler of sort, a vital trait of third places.

Some cafés have seen the commercial potential in this particular group, establishing an infrastructure that is useful for mothers. Nursing rooms and floor-space for the prams are typical examples. In one of the cafés, we counted as many as 24 prams on the floor at the same time, clearly indicating both the social potential for mothers, and the economic potential for the cafés.

Concluding Remarks: The Multiple Café Community

This chapter has first and foremost been an empirical exploration in café behavior. As such it has demonstrated that there are many ways of successfully mastering the craft of being a café guest. We have seen that the guests in the cafés are an extremely diverse group. We have found no clear patterns as far as gender, ethnicity, or age goes. However, we have seen that certain cafés accommodate different groups, for instance, through choice of music or physical planning. We have seen people come alone to have a cup of coffee or to read books for hours. We have seen groups of different sizes coming to the café for all thinkable reasons. We have seen mothers, lovers, friends, and children.

As we set out in this chapter, we framed the question of what a café was in terms of community. How do our observations feed into such a notion? One could perhaps argue, based on our data, that there is no such thing as a café community, that the café is simply an arena where modern, urban human beings can express and enact their personalities, independently from each other. This, however, is far from our argument.

Rather than observe an empty space, a blank canvas where atomic individuals drift in and out without purpose or meaning, our observations and interviews suggest that a term such as "café community" makes sense. This is not the same as saying that all cafés we have observed meet all of Ray Oldenburg's criteria for what a "third space" is. Many cafés do, however, at least to a certain degree serve this function. But what makes them successful as such? In the following, we identify three elements that seem particularly important.

Routine: Is important on many levels. Café guests who routinely meet each other in cafés are important constitutive elements of the café. Routinized revisits quickly turns into a status as regulars, which helps sustain the buzz and tone of the café. We have also seen that other routines are important. For instance, the music played in a café might strengthen the routines of café guests.

Belonging: Is of course closely related to the notion of routine, but a sense of belonging does not require routine. For regulars, routine and belonging are two sides of the same coin. Returning to the same café day after day means that you learn how this particular café works. You might get to know the staff, they might give you a nickname, and they know your "usual" order (cf chapter 6, pp. 118–119). For others, the sense of belonging can be rooted in a more abstract notion of identity, for instance, anchored in the music played, the "atmosphere" of the café, the quality of the coffee served, or an idea about who the others who frequent this particular café are. Belonging might also be related to geography: the fact that a café is located in a certain part of town as opposed to other cafés elsewhere might be part of this. Many social theorists focus on the fragmentation of modern societies, a form of individualization or a turn away from traditional institution. Our interviews and observations suggest that the café might be a new arena where individuals build ontological security (e.g., Giddens, 1990) anchored in a mutual sense of belonging and community.

Public solitude: While routine and belonging might seem like inherently collective qualities, we have seen that one of the most important aspects of cafés as communities is that they allow for public solitude in a way that few, if any other third places do (cf chapter 9). Public solitude opens up for a range of possibilities: it can be disciplining for work and other projects, it may remove some of the urgency from other aspects of life, but it also renders the person in public solitude open to unexpected social engagements.

In this chapter, we have studied the behavior of café guests. Through this exercise we have come to see that it makes sense to talk about the café as a community, constituted both by the behavior of café guests and their experience of the café. While it is unclear what the roles of such communities are in modern societies, we are convinced that they provide an important contribution as societies are reconfigured and strive to find their new shapes in the years to come.

References

Delanty, G. (2003) *Community*. New York: Routledge.
Giddens, A. (1990) *Consequences of Modernity*. Cambridge: Polity Press.
Habermas, J. (1989) *The Structural Transformation of the Public Society. An Inquiry into a Category of Bourgeois Society*. Oxford: Polity Press.
Hampton, K. N. and Gupta, N. (2008) Community and social interaction in the wireless city. Wi-fi use in public and semi-public spaces. *New Media Society*, 10, 831–850.
Holm, E. D. (2010) *Coffee and the City. Towards a Soft Urbanity*. PhD Thesis. Oslo: Arkitekt og designhøyskolen i Oslo.
Oldenburg, R. (1999) *The Great Good Place: Cafés, Coffee Shops, Bookstores, Bars, Hair salons and Other Hangouts at the Heart of a Community*. New York: Marlowe and company.
Tjora, A. (2012) *Kvalitative forskningsmetoder i praksis*. Oslo: Gyldendal.

6

COMMUNAL AWARENESS IN THE URBAN CAFÉ

Aksel Tjora

There is no doubt that cafés and coffee shops are great places to meet friends and colleagues, to chat, plan work, just take a break together, have a coffee obviously, or otherwise be social in the urban facilities that these venues offer. However, the cafés are much more than meeting places; in fact they may be places not to meet, not to talk, not to be social, at least explicitly: they might be places for solitude (cf. chapter 9). My interest in this chapter is with *subtle communal processes*, or what I would like to call *communal awareness* in cafés. While people come to cafés to be alone, just sipping to a coffee by themselves, reading the newspaper or a book, or working by the use of a laptop PC (perhaps connected through a wireless network, cf. chapter 8), my café observations support the idea of a *café sociality* supporting ad hoc chats and a *communal* atmosphere. Using cafés for work or a break in solitude does not therefore undermine these places as social. Rather, the subtleness of *café communities* may challenge the familiar notion of community, both in everyday language and in the social sciences. With this chapter, I apply this challenge from café studies to explore community as situational and place-based, but often subtle. I am curious about how one can understand community on basis of social life in the café. As this is partly a theoretical ambition, I start with a very brief review of the community concept in sociology.

The Concept of Community

It is understandable that the "near-ubiquity" of the term "community" (Cohen, 1985) is matched by the vagueness and variability of it's meaning. The term is used widely in everyday language, often without any particular exact meaning, to leave it to various actors and audiences to make sense of it's content, often specific to a context. This is not at least evident in Norway, after the tragic violent attack on the government buildings and people participating in Labour party's youth camp July 22, 2011. One year running before the incident, the word "community" (fellesskap) was used 15.000 times in the Norwegian paper-based news media, while there are more than 20.000 hits the first year following the incident. Restoring and maintaining a strong sense of (social-democratic) participatory community has grown into a grand national rhetoric during 2011–2012. Although this recent political discourse may have widened the content of the term into an absurd vagueness, I argue that there are many reasons for sociology (and the social sciences in general) to place a more elaborate application of the term (back) into the core of the discipline. With this aim, there is reason to look back into the early history of sociology.

The German sociologist Ferdinand Tönnies has become famous for the terms *Gemeinschaft* and *Gesellschaft*, as two "normal types" (concepts) of human association. Tönnies' concepts were published first in German in 1887 and soon became part of the general stock of concepts that pre-1933 German intellectuals were quite familiar with. Gemeinschaft (often translated as community) is an association in which individuals are oriented to the large association as much as, if not more than, to their own self-interest. Furthermore, individuals in Gemeinschaft are regulated by common beliefs about the appropriate behavior and responsibility of members of the association, to each other and to the association at large; associations are marked by "unity of will." Tönnies saw the family as the most perfect expression of Gemeinschaft; however, he expected that Gemeinschaft could be based on shared place and shared belief as well as kinship, and he included globally dispersed religious communities as possible examples.

In contrast, Gesellschaft (often translated as society, civil society, or association) describes associations in which, for the individual, the larger association never takes precedence over the individual's self interest, and these associations lack the same level of shared belief. Gesellschaft is maintained through individuals acting in their own self interest, like in business life: the workers, managers, and owners may share in very limited ways orientations or beliefs, they may not care deeply for the product they are making, but it is in all their self interest to come to work to make money, and thus continuing business and Gesellschaft relations. Gesellschaft society involves achieved status, by education and work, for example, through the attainment of goals, or attendance at University.

Also Emile Durkheim was concerned with the question of community, for example, in his critique of Tönnies' ideas of Gemeinschaft as organic and Gesellschaft as mechanical (Delanty, 2003: 36). Rather, Durkheim suggested that life in large groups was as natural as life in small groups (1893/1964) and that organic forms of solidarity were replacing a traditional mechanical solidarity in modernity, and also that these forms of solidarity would coexist (Cohen, 1985: 24). Simply stated, mechanical solidarity is the social integration of members of a society who have common values and beliefs, into a kind of "collective consciousness" that works internally in individual members to make them able to cooperate. Durkheim uses the term "mechanic," drawing on a physical science metaphor, to think about people as being connected by internal energies, like those that cause molecules to cohere in a solid. He establishes organic solidarity as a contrast, in which social integration arises out of the need of individuals for one another's services. In a society characterized by organic solidarity, we will find a greater division of labor, with individuals as interdependent but differentiated, as different organs of a living body. Society relies less on imposing uniform rules on everyone and more on regulating the relations between different groups and persons, for example, through the greater use of contracts and laws.

Later, during the 1920s and 1930, the Chicago School of Sociology developed a concern with the growing urbanization and it's social consequences, in Chicago, and developing an ethnographically based urban sociology. Chicago school sociologists saw the city as mosaics of different social milieus that did not interpenetrate (Park, 1915) and networks that were socially distant although physically close (Wirth, 1938). Applying Durkheim's solidarity terms, Chicago school sociologists were concerned with the opposing qualities of the more complex urban community and the less complex rural "folk community." In retrospect, Chicago sociologists such as Robert Park and Louis Wirth may have been too quick to conclude on the complexity of the urban and the simplicity of the rural, as well as applying Durkheim's mechanic and organic solidarity as a historic development rather than as a taxonomy (Cohen, 1985: 29).

More recently, during the last 20 years or so, the question about community has been raised with a growing concern about individualization and a loss of neighborhood relations, with isolation as consequence. In the United States, Robert Putnam successfully promoted the idea of loss of social capital in suburban life with his book *Bowling Alone* (2000). However, Putnam has been criticized both for squeezing too much out of the available quantitative empirical data, for applying the term social capital on a discussion about individualism (Fischer, 2005), and for pushing the "loss" argument too far, and being unable to spot other possible explanations, of "transformation" of community, for instance (cf. Wellman, 1979). As contrasting evidence, international comparative studies show that the amount of voluntary involvement of groups and individual citizens in local-level activities has increased over recent years, thus strengthening social community (Wollmann, 2006: 1432). Furthermore, Delanty (2003: 120) argues that "personal self-fulfilment and individualized expression can be highly compatible with collective participation." On basis of individuated politics based on reflexivity and autonomy, as argued by Giddens (1991) and Beck and Beck-Gernsheim (2002) among others, one may find local community being strengthened by some sort of "collective individualism" (Delanty, 2003: 126). Contemporary communities are therefore groupings that are products of practices rather than structures: "Communities are created rather that reproduced," Delanty (2003: 130) argues, to conclude that these practices consist first of all of communication, or communicative action (Habermas, 1984; 1987) to construct "communication communities."

Another approach to the phenomenon is suggested by Michel Maffesoli, who introduced "neotribes" as another way to look at communities. He is concerned with a "constant interplay between the growing massification and the development of microgroups" (1996: 6), or "tribes." With his concern about sociality, and a sceptisism toward the well-marketed sociological idea of individualism, tribalism is used to denote a "patchwork of small entities" (p. 9), all hold together in a "shared sensibility or emotion" (p. 28). I find the idea of neotribalism interesting because of the emphasis of *sense of community*, developed from submitting to a certain way of life or applying certain symbols and markers. People may participate in a vast range of such communities, or be member of many tribes, at the same time continuously and/or at different occasions. Accordingly, the anthropologist Anthony P. Cohen's emphasis on how communities are constructed through meaning (1985), and not through structures, is relevant here. Cohen suggests that recognizing the other as similar to oneself (more alike than different) is a sense of community (1985: 116).

For a greater concern of the details of how communities are developed and maintained through social praxis, I find the interactionist sociological tradition of *workplace studies* (Heath and Luff, 2000; Luff, Hindmarsh, and Heath, 2000) relevant. Applying ethnomethodological perspectives (Garfinkel, 1967) as basis, such studies elaborate on interactive aspects of work practices, subtle forms of communication, and the way technological systems are applied. The strong focus on situated practice (as opposed to formal plans and structures) is also maintained by Suchman (1987) and Lave and Wenger, the latter by the concept of "communities of practice" (Lave and Wenger, 1991; Wenger, 1998). These studies points to organizations (or other practicing collectives) as self-organizing systems, with many of the benefits and characteristics of associational life such as the generation of what Robert Putnam and others have discussed as social capital (Smith, 2003). Communities of practice are developed through shared practices, people involving themselves in certain common activities and through mutual engagement binding members together as a social entity (Wenger, 1998).

Toward a Sociology of Cafés

Although cafés certainly have large social relevance, for instance, in urban areas, social research on cafés and coffee shops has been surprisingly limited. In addition to George Simmel and Jürgen Habermas, who both have discussed cafés as places in which strangers meet and where a potential for a public sphere is developed, more recent empirical directions include the American sociologist Ray Oldenburg, who analyzed cafés, coffee shops, bookstores, and so on, as "third places" (cf. Oldenburg, 1999; chapter 1), the British researcher Eric Laurier, who has done a fair amount of café studies from a ethnomethodological point of departure (cf. chapter 7), focusing on the everyday "practice" in cafés, and the Swedish sociologist Franz Oddner, who studied café conversations (2003). Oldenburg (1999) is concerned about the loss of meeting places in residential areas in the United States and demonstrates the state of affairs in current American suburbia by contrasting this to his analyses of German beer gardens, English pubs, French cafés, and classic European coffeehouses, as well as historical accounts of pre-1940's American small-town main streets and taverns (cf. chapters 3 and 4). Eric Laurier and Chris Philo have published work as part of the "Cappucino Community" ESRC project (Laurier, 2005a), in which they use ethnomethodology (Garfinkel, 1967) as framework for analyses of how customers, owners, and personnel maintain various social occasions that in sum define what the café *is*. Phenomena such as encounters between strangers or "familiar strangers"

(Laurier and Philo, 2006), closing of coffee conversations (Laurier, 2008a), the time-space properties of crowds during café breakfast (Laurier, 2008b), sequences of café customer "practices" (Laurier, 2005b), social-material organization of space, informality, and rule-following (Laurier, Whyte, and Buckner, 2001), various types of cafés (Laurier, 2004) as well as what it requires to be a barista (Laurier, 2003; chapter 7), have been studied.

Spanning from the role of the café in the neighborhood (Oldenburg) to the very detailed interactive practices that we find in cafés (Laurier), it is obvious that *café sociology* must be diverse exercise. While Oldenburg is concerned with the social life (talk, support, and so on), one of my main interests is with the more immediate, but less explicit sense of café community. Even when a café is not tied to specific physical already existing communities, it may still develop as a source of community on basis of communication rather than geography/location. And further, I suggest that it makes sense to include also the very subtle forms of communication that we find well described by interactionist sociologists such as Erving Goffman (1959, 1963), including short glances and careful inattentive acknowledgements, as communication. Hence, the term "awareness," as used within sociology of organizations, CSCW,[1] and "workplace studies," becomes relevant for the subtle communal practices in cafés, that is, *communal awareness.*

Especially within the above-mentioned "workplace studies," a number of concepts have been suggested, that in various ways are related to awareness (Dourish and Bellotti, 1992; Schmidt, 2002), such as *participation frameworks* (Suchman, 1996), *legitimate peripheral participation* (Lave and Wenger, 1991), *socially distributed cognition* (Hutchins, 1990; 1995; Hutchins and Klausen, 1996; Raeithel, 1996; Star, 1996), and *attention* (Tjora, 2004a). With the emphasis on intense collaborative work situations, studies within this tradition has often been concerned with how information is widely distributed in various ways, without experiencing *redundancy* as problem but as a resource (Cabitza et al., 2005; Landau, 1969; Tjora,

1997, 2004a), for example, in providing *action alternatives*. I suggest in this analysis that such action alternatives in workplace studies may be reframed as *communal potential* in studies of cafés and coffeehouses. I suggest that it makes sense to argue for a relation between workplace studies' emphasis on subtleness in coordinating activities and the idea of modern communities as *communication communities* (Delanty, 2003).

METHODS: SOFT-EXPERIMENTAL AUTO-ETHNOGRAPHY

My research into café communities has been supported by a group of research assistants, to perform observation and spontanuous interviews in a wide range of cafés and coffee shops (cf. chapter 5). While this chapter has been informed by this wider *café sociology project*, its empirical basis is however limited to my own individual observation as full participant (Gold, 1958) in four cafés in four different cities in three different continents in the period between 2007 and 2011. I have applied a plain observation and note-taking, as well as a "soft-experimental" auto-ethnographic design,[2] in which I enter a café, which I have previously never visited, in a town in which I am mainly a stranger, and spend significantly amount of café time on a daily basis over a period of at least two weeks. The idea is to study communal experiences in a fresh place, in which I am nothing than just any other customer. I do what any other "normal" customer do, order my coffee, find a table, use my laptop to work,[3] while sipping coffee and every now and then raising my head watching others, get a sandwich by lunchtime, and so on. The idea of using oneself as an experimental unit is not new within human sciences. One of the most fascinating examples is probably Stratton's cognitive-psychological experiment through which he went around with inverting glasses to study visual perception and the impact of previous experience (Stratton, 1896). A much more recent autobigraphical turn within anthropology (cf. Okely and Callaway, 1992) has also promoted the relevance of applying researcher experiences as valid data in ethnography.

The idea of my study here was conceived during a research sabbatical in the Australian city of Melbourne in 2003, where I found myself experimenting with experiences of homeliness/belonging in various cafés and pubs. Since I was spending day-time in cafés, and using my laptop to work, there were no barriers toward taking small notes of café situations and experiences. When I was back in the same city for another sabbatical in 2007, I went for a more rigid design, detailed note-taking, and the soft-experimental approach. Field studies from the following café cases have been applied in this chapter:

- *AMP: A Minor Place* (studied 2007): A residential area independent neighorhood café in the Brunswick area of Melbourne, serving high quality sandwiches and coffee, breakfast/lunch, and catering all kinds of people, self-employed, students, housewives, families, etc.
- *KCB: Kaffekompaniet Carl Berner* (studied 2008): An urban not-so-fancy area neighborhood café in Oslo, Norway, part of a local chain of cafés, serving sandwiches, coffee, as well as bear and wine, open from early morning till late evening, catering unemployed and pensioners, self-employed, local business lunchers, workers, immigrants, etc.
- *KBS: Kaffebønna Stortorget* (studied 2009–2011): A mid-city stylish independent[4] café in Tromsø, Norway, serving home-baked pastries and high-quality coffee,[5] catering the creative middle class for morning coffee and lunch, as well as any occasional city shopper.
- *SCH: Sack's Coffee House* (studied 2011): A quite large local residential/small-business area café in Berkeley's Elmwood village (California), serving home-made soups, bagels and sandwiches, and good coffees and teas, catering students, academics, and self-employed, of which a majority sit alone with their laptop.

The selected cafés are all well-run, popular places, with an emphasis on good coffee and lunch-style food, and catering a wide range of people and groups. They are crowded with people in solitude, ususally working or doing some sort of individual activity, as well as people in pairs, a family now and then, and other groups of people. All the cafés are equipped with wireless Internet, and using a laptop is well accepted, which makes note-taking easy.

Analysis 1: Interacting Community

In my observation during my café studies, I am concerned with situations and how they unfold. Submitting to the interactionist position of Strauss (1978; 1993), I argue that community is developed and maintained (performed) through various practices of café users (customers and employees). During my observation studies, I am therefore strongly concerned with action and interaction, or, to be true to Strauss (1993) *acting* and *interacting*, not only to suggest that these processes *produce* community but also that these processes *are* community. My curiosity is in other words aimed at a nuanced inductive analysis of the various processes through which community is *enacted*.

During my field studies in the above-mentioned cafés I have identified 5 different *communal interactings*, (1) recognizing the other, (2) experiencing situations together, (3) perceiving the other's needs, (4) trusting the other, and (5) showing and accepting curiosity. I briefly present these.

Recognizing the Other

Recognition is a process both between the personnel (baristas and waiters) and customers and between customers.

> *KCB: The morning coffee*
> Barista (to the male customer as he approaches the counter at the far end from the entrance of the café.): "So, you're here for the morning coffee?"
> *Customer*: "Yes, I am."
> And the barista makes a double latte, without the customer specifying his order.
> ⎯
> *KBS: A male Cortado drinker*

Barrista: Hi there (to the entering customer, in a recognizing manner) – Cortado?
Customer (while taking off his coat and placing a laptop on a table): Cortado! (confirming).

KBS: Suggesting a bonus card
Barista (serving coffee to a customer): Don't you have a bonus card?
Customer: I suppose I should have...
Barista: Yeah, *you* should have one!

In the first extract, the expression "the morning coffee" and not only "a coffee" or "a coffee this morning" confirms the barista's recognition of the customer's habit of having the same coffee every morning. Suggesting a Cortado in the second excerpt serves the same purpose, underlining the barista's knowledge about a customer's regular routine. In the third situation, the barista underlines that this particular customer is one of those who should have a bonus card, obviously (on the basis of barista's knowledge) being one of the regulars.

Also, the customer may initiate the interaction pointing toward recognizing the barista.

KCB: Complimenting the barista's hair-do
Male customer (to the female barista as she is preparing his coffee): "You're hair is really looking good today."
Barista: "Yeah, but it's too long."

Referring to the barista's hairdo makes obvious that the customer knows about her hair the day(s) before. Also between the regular customers, acts of recognizing the other is evident from situations:

KCB: Being haughty
Woman (on her way out of the door, almost passing a male customer, who is seated just by the door, but turns back to him): "Hi there, didn't mean to be haughty."
Man: "Hi, yeah, but that's what you are" (ironically)
Woman: "I'm in a hurry..."
Man: nodding, smiling back at her, as she walks out the door.

The woman acknowledges the fact that she *breaches* the rule of explicitly recognizing and greeting the other regular, and tries to *repair* the situation (as described by Garfinkel (1967) and Goffman (1963)), which is accepted, by an ironic response and a smile.

These "recognition interactings" are performed continuously between people in all kinds of (social) circumstances. They may be subtle (smiles and nods) or explicit, like the small episodes above, but they are all core performances within the sociality of cafés. In some situations, they may develop into informal chats or confirmation of a common experience.

Experiencing Situations Together

Another communal process is related to experiencing a situation together. In the Norwegian climate, the straightforwardly shared experience of weather conditions is a very common topic for informal chats.

> *KCB*: *Cold weather*
> Female customer (in her mid 60s, at the counter): "It was cold today!"
> *Barista*: "Yes, it was."
> *Customer*: "Only 3 degrees [Celsius] this morning!"
> *Barista*: "Wow, it was *that* cold?"
> *Customer*: "Yes,"
> *Barista*: "You know, it was 25 degrees in the sun this weekend."
> *Customer*: "Yeah, let's see if it's better the 17th of May."[6]

The weather situation is a very safe common ground for a chat between most Norwegians (both familiar and strangers), and in that sense an interaction pretext (Henriksen and Tjora, 2013; Tjora, Henriksen, Fjærli, and Grønning, 2012), on basis of which talk is legitimized. As opposed to happenings, like a football match or a concert that triggers a "focused attention" (Tjora, 2004b), a general topic like the weather works for any informal chat (or for initiating a chat) between Norwegians. Next, I show how visible problems or needs are other bases for interaction.

Perceiving the Other's Needs

With a general (subtle) orientation toward each other in the café, needs (or problems or challenges) may be observable and potentially trigger action:

> *SCH: Searching for power*
> A woman around the age of 22 is looking around, behind tables, toward walls.
> Man (noticing the woman's searching): "You're looking for some power plugs?"
> *Woman:* "yeah."
> Man (pointing): "they're right over there."
> The woman finds a table that makes her able to plug her Macbook to the wall.
>
> ---
>
> *AMP: Giving me the password*
> It is my day 2 at AMP, and the woman with a laptop that I spoke to the first day approaches me to share the password for the Wi-Fi network, which she now has got from the café staff.

The extensive use of laptops in cafés (cf. chapter 8) is quite often not well reflected in the availability of power outlets, and the lack of these has become an interesting common challenge in many cafés, and a source of assistance between café customers. I have observed people pointing out possible outlets for each other (like the example above), as well as sharing such outlets (or power adapters) so that nobody runs out of battery. Sharing passwords, solving each other's Wi-Fi connection problems, as well as charging mobile phones and laptops are common challenges, but at the same time triggers of communal interacting. Using expensive technological equipment (e.g., laptops) in cafés also demonstrates another aspect, that of trust.

Trusting the Other

During my many hours spent in the four case cafés, and more or less any other café, the degree of trust between customers is striking. Especially the relaxed leaving-behind stuff on the table is a confirmation of this.

SCH: A woman aged around 26 seated just beside me, leaves her laptop and mobile phone on the table and walks to the restroom. We have not been communicating, as she has been sitting with her iPod earplugs in all the time, alone, leaving everything on the table without any eye contact and communication whatsoever.

AMP: I come in about 11 in the morning and have a coffee while working on my laptop. After a while I get hungry, order another coffee and a "Xanadu" (open toasted sandwich with cottage cheese, tomato, avocado, rocket, dukkah, and pesto oil), but I am out of cash, and since the café do not accept cards, I ask for the closest ATM (being not far away), and asking two of the women at the community table if they "would be there the next ten minutes." They understand that I am in fact asking them to look after my stuff, including the laptop, they nod implicitly looking toward my stuff ("yes, we will look after it for you"), and I go on my bike.

SCH: The woman by the table beside me walks to the bathroom, and afterwards directly out of the café, leaving laptop and glasses on the table. We catch each other's eyes as she leaves the café at 11:59, to return at 12.12, and then sitting down at her table again without making any comments or signs, and replugging her music.

My interest with this kind of trust is how it seems to be produced immediately, between total strangers, just by being customer in the same specific café, and not necessarily on basis of any other kind of familiarity. I have been observing a vast range of variations of leaving things on café tables, between asking people nearby to look after things explicitly, to not even making any gestures toward "table-neighboring" customers before leaving things behind. Sack's Coffee House in Berkeley is crowded with laptop workers (cf. also chapter 8), and it seems to be taken for granted that laptops and mobile phones being left behind should be looked after by table neighbors (or a more general café community?). My suggestion is that an immediate trust between strangers is part of the communal awareness in cafés.

Showing and Accepting Curiosity

One of the most interesting processes of communal awareness is based on what we might call *legitimate curiosity*:

> *SCH*: "Oh, an iPad keyboard?", one customer asks one of the other, "never seen that one before, is it specially for the iPad?", and a conversation about this evolves.
>
> *AMP*: I am on my way on the bike passing someone sitting outside the neighborhood café *A Minor Place* with a Titan laptop, and I stop my bike, to ask her if there is a Wi-Fi Internet connection there. She tells me that there is, although she experiences trouble getting connection at that specific time. It seems to be a good place for a coffee, and I lock my bike and enter[7].
>
> *AMP*: A man on my own age sits beside me (by the community table) practising sign writing. After having observed him for a while I ask him which language he is practising (I guess Japanese or Chinese). He tells me it is Japanese; and those of the Japanese sign language that is closest related to Chinese, and further that there are three sign alphabets in Japanese and that the two other are traditionally masculine vs feminine. He asks me where I am from (having an accent) and I tell him I am from Norway, being on a sabbatical at LaTrobe University, but spending some days in cafés to do work. He has studied at LaTrobe himself, and we approach the topic of libraries, the joy of libraries, those at LaTrobe and Melbourne University, and so on.

Curiosity from the other occasional café customer is legitimized by a novel practice or product (the keyboard) or something that is accepted as widely useful and easily sharable (a Wi-Fi network). In the latter excerpt, we approach a whole range of ad hoc themes of common interest, just on basis of ending up beside each other at the community table, and after my curiosity with the sign writing.

Communal Processes as Community

Applying an interactionist approach to community I am concerned with how situations as the above mentioned are on one hand taken-for-granted social norms (with surprisingly little variations between my cases), and on the other hand those processes that a "café community" consists of. As a very committed café ethnographer with a strong interactionist sympathy, I put heavy emphasis on these episodes to be able to explore the details of a café society. In the next section, I apply a more auto-ethnographical approach to explore the experience of becoming a regular.

ANALYSIS 2: BECOMING ONE OF THE REGULARS

One of the most interesting communal processes can be experienced by making rotuine visits to a café that is new to the researcher, applying what I call a soft-experimental approach. The method requires extensive note-taking, and a persistent attitude, but is rewarding over time. To be able to experience how the café and its employees influence ones own "regularness," it is important to keep to routines. Although I was not able to maintain a "time-routine," I was always ordering the same coffee (a strong skinny[8]) and picking a seat by the same community table. The following excerpt sketches very briefly some of my experiences during daily visits to *A Minor Place* (AMP) in Melbourne (only a few of the days are reported from).

> *Day 8*: I arrive at 09:15, there are 5–6 people there. The waitress behind the counter greets me especially nice, with an obvious recognition ("Hi, how are you?"). At 10:30, I am about to leave, to check out Caffe Alleri (another favorite place), but one of the waiters asks me if I want another coffee, and as always when being asked, I say "Yes, please," and he responds "another strong skinny?"
>
> *Day 9*: I come in at 09:35, approaching the counter, as one of the waitresses just outside it greets me: "Hi, how are you?" (I: Good, good). "Would you like a coffee?" (I am nodding).

"Strong skinny?", she asks me, and I feel like getting to a next level of becoming "one of the regulars." I place myself at the community table, as usual.

Day 10: I come in at 09:35, walk over to the counter: "Hi, I would like a coffee, a strong skinny one." Waiter: "a latte?" Me: "yes, please." He: "Over there at the big table?" I nod to confirm—it is where I always sit, and this has been recognized.

Day 13: I come in at 13:30, walk to the counter, standing looking at the board behind, with lunches and breakfasts, struggling to make a decision. "A skinny strong latte?" the barista asks me. "Yes, thanks. And I have to decide for some lunch" asking for a suggestion. Later that day, in a *bottle shop* in another neighborhood, I meet the "Titan woman" that I had met at day 2 (giving me the password for the AMP Wi-Fi network, mentioned above). We greet each other, like any other acquaintances.

Day 14: I come in at 13:20. Almost before I enter, one of the waitresses (who I can't remember having been there much) just says "Hi, strong skinny latte? Won't be a minute."

Day 16: I come in at 08:15. The waiter: "Early in today?" Me: "Yeah, [must] try to do some work." While I am sitting there the Titan-woman comes in, and we greet each other.

Day 17: I come in at 08.10. Waiter: "Strong skinny?" Me: "Yes, please." After having emptied it, one of the waitresses observes my empty cup, asking "Another coffee, strong skinny?" I go to the university and comes back after a while, ordering a muffin and a long black, and the waitress, with surprise, has to ask once more: "Long black?"

During a period of three weeks I visited *A Minor Place* on a daily basis, experiencing the café very quickly as a familiar place, feeling at home just after very few days, and being confirmed as "one of the regulars"—the ninth day the waitress taking for granted my "routine" coffee and the tenth day the barista suggesting where I would like to sit. In fact, having to leave Melbourne to go back to Norway after three weeks of daily visits in the café, felt like leaving a group of friends, and I felt a need to thank the personnel for the good time and apologize for discontinuing my regular visits.

Discussion

In this chapter, I am concerned with developing the term *communal awareness*, from communal processes identified during observation in the four case cafés. Maintaining a strong *inductive* and *constructivist-interactionist* approach, I have put emphasis on how community are constructed and experienced through interaction. In the previous sections, I have identified 5 communal processes (interactings); (1) recognizing the other (2) experiencing situations together, (3) perceiving the other's needs, (4) trusting the other, and (5) showing and accepting curiosity. I have also explored a more longitudinally based experience of becoming one of the regulars. In approaching the phenomenon of community through microsociological ethnography, that is, by directly observable (explicit) interactions and own experiences, I do not argue that my synthesis of communal processes is encompassing. However, I will claim that my analysis represent a valid *conceptual generalization* (Tjora, 2012) of relevance for a more nuanced sociological exploration of community, in public and semi-public spaces.

The nuances of communal processes and experiences stand in some contrast to the concepts of Tönnies and Dürkheim, who were concerned about dichotomies such as gemeinschaft/gesellschaft and mechanic/organic solidarity. However, as we think of these dichotomies less as description of historical development, but as ideal types to identify parallel sources of community and solidarity (Cohen, 1985), the concepts are highly relevant for the café community. In the analysis above, it is evident that baristas and waiters (the professionals) are core actors in the processes of becoming recognized as one of the regulars. It is part of their job. Also evident is the role of interaction between various guests (or customers) to develop and maintain communal sensibility and trust. Hence, business-based (gesellschaft) and ad hoc informal (gemeinschaft) interactions (and relations) do both construct the café society.

Applying a social network perspective, and the emphasis on weak "social ties" enabling access to potential resources within distant networks (Granovetter, 1973), we may suggest "subtle ties" as less explicit "social resources" being developed and maintained in cafés (Tjora and Scambler, 2009). One of Granovetter's arguments is that weak ties demand low investments in maintenance and that one actor therefore is capable of maintaining a vast number of such social ties, and with potential to access a wide range of resources. While weak ties are personally specific, including named acquaintances, neighbors, colleagues, distant family, and so on, subtle ties are unnamed and based on recognition from having a third place in common. Greeting the "Titan lady" that I recognized from A Minor Place, when I met her at a bottle shop in another end of town, is one result of subtle ties. They do not necessarily provide access to resources (which is one on Granovetter's interests, working within economic sociology), but may strengthen a feeling of being part of social networks (increased social capital) and experiencing ontological security (Giddens, 1991). While a network perspective provides an important reflection on resources generated on basis of prolonged use of cafés, it does not however contribute to a more nuanced exploration of the actual social processes within them. For a more detailed discussion of these processes, I have found ethnomethodologially oriented organization studies, that is, "workplaces studies," to do so.

Through analysis of control rooms and similar intensive collaborative work situations, workplace studies are concerned with detailed analyses of processes of handling and sharing information, and coordinating action, developing concepts such as "multiple, interacting participating frameworks" (Suchman, 1993), "peripheral participation" (Lave and Wenger, 1991), and "socially distributed cognition" (Hutchins, 1995). In my studies of medical emergency call centres, I have been especially interested in how operators combine an "overall attention" (to all on-going actions in the centre) with a "focused attention" (to individual work tasks) to produce a service that is both resilient and flexible (Tjora, 2004b). Overall attention is closely related to the concept "awareness" that has been widely applied and redeveloped within workplace studies and CSCW research, although its popularity has led to its equivocality, and it being used in increasingly contradictory ways (Schmidt, 2002). While I have suggested *overall attention* to be used for the *active* observation and engagement in the activity of other people, *awareness* suggests an understanding of the activities of others as a *context* for one's own activity (Dourish & Bellotti, 1992), that is, in a somewhat more passive way.

In the cafés, both my observation of the interaction between regulars, between customers and baristas, as well as my experience of becoming one of the regulars point in the direction of a form of awareness; what I would like to term *communal awareness*. Café customers drink coffee, eat lunch, work on their laptops, chat, read, etc. in the context of others' reading, eating, etc. Being aware of one of the other's hunt for a power outlet, a password, or needing the stuff looked after during a little visit to the men's room are expressions of communal awareness. The experience of communal awareness is a true experience of community; it is community because it is experienced as such (Cohen, 1985; Thomas and Thomas, 1928). It is community although it is not as explicitly performed through jovial chats and social encounters as Oldenburg's "third places" (chapter 1). It is community on basis of people's recognition of each other as regular users of the same café, or belonging to the same *café tribe* (to give a twist on Maffesoli, 1996).

In developing the concept communal awareness I argue that communities are developed and experienced through microinteraction in cafés and other places where people meet. With inspiration from Cohen (1985), I suggest that *experiences* of community must be studied to be able to identify community and that social gatherings and explicit communication are not necessary prerequisites for a café society. With an increasing number of cafés and coffee shops, at least in many urban communities, there is hope for a developed and maintained communal awareness. More detailed research work is however needed to better understand the wider meaning and impact of social life in such cafés. For the potential prosperity of communal life, both in urban and rural societies, a more thorough knowledge of the societal relevance of awareness and interaction in the café society must be sought for.

Notes

1. Computer-supported cooperative work.
2. By using the term "soft-experiment," I refer to an experimental orientation, that is, imposing a change (my own changed behavior – spending much time in a new café) for the purpose of doing research, but in a "soft" way, that is, not imposing actual changes in research subjects (doing just what every other café customer do).
3. In all the cafés visited working with laptops is wide-spread.
4. The local company runs two cafés.
5. Baristas from Kaffebønna compete successfully in Barista Art championships.
6. The Norwegian National Day.
7. This incident represents the start of a more systematic café sociology, by my first visit to A Minor Place.
8. A "strong skinny" is Melbourne slang for a double (strong) latte with skimmed milk (skinny). It is served in quite small glasses and will be very close to a Cortado in most European cafés.

References

Beck, U. and Beck-Gernsheim. (2002) *Individualization*. London: Sage.
Cabitza, F., et al. (2005) *When Once Is Not Enough: The Role of Redundancy in a Hospital Ward Setting*. Paper presented at the GROUP'05, Sanibel Island, Florida, USA.
Cohen, A. P. (1985) *The Symbolic Construction of Community*. London: Routledge.
Delanty, G. (2003) *Community*. London: Routledge.
Dourish, P. and Bellotti, V. (1992) *Awareness and Coordination in Shared Workspaces*. Paper presented at the CSCW 92.
Durkheim, E. (1893/1964). *The Division of Labour in Society*. Glencoe: The Free Press.
Fischer, C. S. (2005) Bowling alone: what's the score. Book review of Robert Putnam: Bowling Alone. *Social Networks*, 27, 155–167.
Garfinkel, H. (1967) *Studies in Ethnometholodology*. Cambridge: Polity Press.
Giddens, A. (1991) *Modernity and Self-Identity: Self and Society in the Late Modern Age*. Cambridge: Polity Press.
Goffman, E. (1959) *The Presentation of Self in Everyday Life*. New York: Doubleday.
Goffman, E. (1963) *Behaviour in Public Places*. New York: The Free Press.

Gold, R. R. (1958) Sociological field observations. *Social Forces*, 36, 217–223.
Habermas, J. (1984) *The Theory of Comminicative Action* (Vol. 1: Reason and the Rationalization of Society). London: Heinemann.
Habermas, J. (1987). *The Theory of Communicative Action* (Vol. 2: Lifeworld and System: A Critique of Functionalist Reason). Cambridge: Polity Press.
Heath, C. and Luff, D. (2000) *Technology in Action*. Cambridge: Cambridge University Press.
Henriksen, I. M. and Tjora, A. (2013) Interaction Pretext: Experiences of Community in the Urban Neighbourhood. *Urban Studies*.
Hutchins, E. (1990) The Technology of Team Navigation. In Galegher, J., Krauss, R. M., and Egido, C. (Eds) *Intellectual Teamwork: Social and Technological Foundations of Cooperative Work*. Hillsdale, NJ: Lawrence Erlbaum Associates.
Hutchins, E. (1995) *Cognition in the Wild*. Cambridge, MA: MIT Press.
Hutchins, E. and Klausen, T. (1996) Distributed Cognition in an Airline Cockpit. In Engeström and Middleton (Eds) *Cognition and Communication at Work*. Cambridge: Cambridge University Press, pp. 15–34.
Landau, M. (1969) Redundancy, rationality, and the problem of duplication and overlap. *Public Administration Review*, 27, 346–358.
Laurier, E. (2003) *Field Report 1: The Basics of Becoming a Barista*. Glasgow: Department of Geography, University of Glasgow.
Laurier, E. (2004) *Field Report 2: One or Several Cafés: An Ethnographic Report*. Glasgow: Department of Geography, University of Glasgow.
Laurier, E. (2005a) *ESRC Final Report: The Cappucino Community: Cafés and Civic Life in the Contemporary City*. Glasgow: University of Glasgow.
Laurier, E. (2005b) *Field Report 3: What Café Customers Do*. Glasgow: Department of Geography, University of Glasgow.
Laurier, E. (2008a) Drinking up endings: conversational resources of the café. *Language & Communication*, 28(2), 165–181.
Laurier, E. (2008b) How breakfast happens in the café. *Time & Society*, 17(1), 119–143.
Laurier, E. and Philo, C. (2006) Possible geographies: a passing encounter in a café. *Human Geography*, 38(4), 353–363.
Laurier, E., Whyte, A., and Buckner, K. (2001) An ethnography of a neighbourhood café: informality, table arrangements and background noise. *Journal of Mundane Behaviour*, 2(2).
Lave, J. and Wenger, E. (1991) *Situated Learning: Legitimate Peripheral Participation*. Cambridge: Cambridge University Press.

Luff, P., Hindmarsh, J., and Heath, C. (Eds) (2000) *Workplace Studies: Recovering Work Practice and Informing System Design.* Cambridge: Cambridge University Press.
Maffesoli, M. (1996) *The Time of the Tribes: The Decline of Individualism in Mass Society.* London: Sage.
Oddner, F. (2003) *Kafékultur, kommunikation och gränser.* Lund: Lund dissertations in Sociology.
Okely, J. and Callaway, H. (Eds) (1992) *Anthropology and Autobiography.* London: Routledge.
Oldenburg, R. (1999) *The Great Good Place* (Third Edn). New York: Marlowe and Company.
Park, R. E. (1915) The city: suggestions for the investigation of human behavior in the city environment. *American Journal of Sociology,* 20(5), 577–612.
Putnam, R. (2000) *Bowling Alone: The Collapse and Revival of American Community.* New York: Simon & Schuster.
Raeithel, A. (1996) On the Ethnography of Cooperative Work. In Engeström and Middleton (Eds) Cognition and Communication at Work. Cambridge: Cambridge University Press, pp. 319–339.
Schmidt, K. (2002) The Problem with 'Awareness.' *Computer Supported Cooperative Work,* 11, 285–298.
Smith, M. K. (2003, 21.06.2006) Communities of practice. *The encyclopedia of informal education.* Retrieved 20.03.2007, 2003, from http://www.infed.org/biblio/communities_of_practice.htm.
Star, S. L. (1996) Working Together: Symbolic Interactionism, Activity Theory, and Information Systems. In Engeström and Middleton (Eds) Cognition and Communication at Work. Cambridge: Cambridge University Press, pp. 296–318.
Stratton, G. M. (1896) Some preliminary experiments on vision without inversion of the retinal image. *Psychological Review,* 3(6), 611–617.
Strauss, A. (1978) *Negotiations.* San Fransisco: Jossey-Bass.
Strauss, A. (1993) *Continual Permutations of Action.* New York: Aldine de Gruyter.
Suchman, L. A. (1987) *Plans and Situated Actions: The Problem of Human-Machine Communication.* Cambridge: Cambridge University Press.
Suchman, L. A. (1993) Technologies of Accountability: of Lizards and Aeroplanes. In Button, G. (Ed.) *Technology in Working Order: Studies of Work, Interaction and Technology.* London: Routledge, pp. 113–126.
Suchman, L. A. (1996) Constituting Shared Workspaces. In Engeström and Middleton (Eds) *Cognition and Communication at Work.* Cambridge UK: Cambridge University Press, pp. 35–60.

Thomas, W. I. and Thomas, D. S. (1928) *The Child in America: Behavior Problems and Programs.* New York: Knopf.
Tjora, A. (1997) *Caring Machines: Emerging Practices of Work and Coordination in the Use of Medical Communication Technology.* (Dr. Polit. (PhD) Thesis), Trondheim: Norwegian University of Science and Technology.
Tjora, A. (2004a) Maintaining redundancy in the coordination of medical emergencies. Paper presented at the CSCW'04, Chicago.
Tjora, A. (2004b) Maintaining redundancy in the coordination of medical emergencies. *CHI Letters,* 6(3), 132–141.
Tjora, A. (2012) *Kvalitative forskningsmetoder i praksis* (second edn). Oslo: Gyldendal Akademisk.
Tjora, A., et al. (2012) *Sammen i byen. En sosiologisk analyse av urbane naboskap, nærmiljø og boligens betydning.* Trondheim: Tapir akademisk.
Tjora, A. and Scambler, G. (2009) *Subtle ties: communal awareness in the urban café.* Paper presented at the BSA annual conference, Cardiff.
Wellman, B. (1979) The community question: intimate networks of East Yorkers. *American Journal of Sociology,* 84, 1201–1231.
Wenger, E. (1998) *Communities of Practice: Learning, Meaning, and Identity.* Cambridge: Cambridge University Press.
Wirth, L. (1938) Urbanism as a way of life. *American Journal of Sociology,* 44(1), 1–24.
Wollmann, H. (2006) The fall and rise of the local community: a comparative and historical perspective. *Urban Studies,* 43(8), 1419–1438.

7

Becoming a Barista

Eric Laurier

Skill and the Barista

It is a perennial feature of low-status jobs such as shop assistants, bar staff, and café baristas that those who do them tend not to stay very long doing them. There is thus a constant entry and exit from the population of this part of the workforce. Nevertheless, the millions of cafés around the world that make espresso by hand need competent, and in some cases excellent, baristas to make their coffee day in, day out. Without competent baristas making consistent coffee, a café will soon lose its reputation and ultimately its custom. It is then a routine requirement of each café that it reproduces the team of workers who are able to make the company's product.

What I want to consider in this chapter is the nature of the ubiquitous skills of making and serving coffees as a barista. Rather than look for general theories of skill that remove it from the particular workplace, tools and contingencies of the job, I want instead to try and reveal what the skills are for this particular culture of catering as it is done in a particular place. Doug Harper (1987) meditated in two part on the skills of a rural mechanic. The first part on just what work of that mechanic was in disassembling, repairing, and rebuilding and, in the second part, on how nevertheless that was woven into relationships the rural community. What I will do here is borrow that structure to consider just what the work of a barista is in making an espresso-based drink and then turning to that task's insertion into the order of service in a café. There are important aspects of serving coffee that diverge from repairing cars and other machines. As Dant (2005) notes automation has not crept into car repair because of the complexity of diagnosis, the "tasks involved, and particularly the wide range of objects that must be interacted with" (p. 135). Making espresso coffee is the perfect contrast case, automation has run riot with tiny pod-based machines for home production and hefty commercial machines that pump out multiple orders and kinds of coffees. Their buttons are backlit and their coffees are often more consistent than the handmade efforts of baristas at manual espresso machines. My ambition here though is not to examine deskilling or indeed, as Ingold (2000) notes, the shift into new skills that is attendant upon automation of earlier routine tasks. What is worth noting though is that the café sector in the the United States and the United Kingdom is anyway giving birth to a "third wave" of cafés that both, continue a longer tradition of artisan roasting and brewing, and converge with customers escaping from global brands and seeking out better quality coffee (Manzo, 2010).

"Skill" as a word carries much less intellectual heft than "mind," never quite right to join the "intellectualist legend" identified by Ryle (2009). Livingston points out that in studying skills all many of us will treat it as "possessed by individuals rather than belonging to a collectivity of practitioners" (Livingston, 2008: 201). Although what might seem striking about Livingston's investigations into skill is the absence of practitioners from the scenes of skill acquisition in playing draughts and doing mathematics that he describes. Why they are missing is because Livingston is continuing the tradition of ethnomethodological studies of reasoning begun by Garfinkel and others (Garfinkel and Rawls, 2002). These studies are warranted by Garfinkel's complaint about Becker's (1996) sociological studies of jazz concentrating on the their relationships as "outsiders" to "squares" and missing the central activity that constitutes the jazz itself, the "missing what" of jazz (Lynch, 1993). A complaint that Becker, always a fellow traveller with ethnomethodology responded to 40 years later with a full-scale study of just that (Faulkner and Becker, 2009). Returning to Livingston's study of skill, it is found in a toolic domain of embodied skills that is distinctive to, and arises from, games, puzzles, and mathematics when we are learning them.

Let me depart from discussing arguments over the nature of skill for a while and turn toward what might be distinctive to, and about, making an espresso in a café. What follows is a task that you will learn more about by replicating, but to do so will require the painful expense of buying a domestic espresso machine or begging one off a well-heeled or coffee-obsessed friend. For my part it was part of a research project of the then new and booming café sector in the United Kingdom (Laurier & Philo, 2005) that provided the opportunity to learn the basic of brewing an espresso.

Instructions + Following Instructions

Commercial coffee machines are built to blast out hundreds of cups a day, consuming litres of water from a mains plumbing supply, having a steam wand at each end, rows of buttons in between levers and dials. They are machines capable of churning out eight single espressos at a time if need be and this does happen in places like Italian railway stations at rush hour. Because it is the size of a toppled drinks cabinet it is all too easy to assume that the espresso machine's operation is central to the creation of a cup of coffee and miss its sister machine: the grinder.

The over-riding fact is that no matter how wonderfully large and matt black the coffee machine, if it does not have properly ground, dosed, and tamped coffee, it will never make "un buon café." As a trainee, I demonstrated that point amply by making runs of substandard espressos, even though two of the key variables are sorted out for the trainee in advance by the trainer: the fineness of the grind and weight of coffee dispensed (7 gm) by my trainer. As part of the institutional structuring, the calibration of fineness and quantity of coffee dispensed is done by experienced staff, generally the manager or their assistant, so in such a situation this is a contingency with which beginner baristas do not have to deal.

Here are the instructions that I was given for you to follow if you have your espresso machine ready (remembering it takes at least half an hour to heat up the machine evenly). In this short chapter, we only deal with espresso and not heating milk for cappuccinos, lattes etc.

1. See if there is enough ground coffee in the doser, if not grind more but not so much that you will leave it sitting in the doser for longer than an hour;
2. Pinch the lever on the doser to dispense the coffee grounds into the portafilter;
3. Tap the handle on the counter to settle the grounds;
4. Press the grounds flat with tamper;
5. Wipe the top of the portafilter clean;
6. Insert the portafilter into the espresso machine and twist it until it is tight;
7. Place cup(s) under it;
8. Press the 2 cup button, or if doing manual timing, run the hot water through for about 25 seconds and then stop;
9. Serve immediately.

Reading these instructions is of quite a different nature to following them, and it is very easy to mistake the ease of reading for a similar ease in following. Ethnomethodological studies have examined the quite different nature of reading instructions as part of following those instructions (Bjelić, 2003; 1995, Liberman 2013). One noticeable thing is that you will inevitably find yourself returning to the instructions to look at them again for what more they might provide in the light of the problems you have encountered trying to make a first cup of coffee. Even once you are able to correctly remember each step of make the espresso, what you fill find, it was certainly what I despaired over, was that the espresso was inconsistent. Sometimes thin and bitter, other times thick and barely a dash of it produced. Why?

Troubles + Hints

The answer is discovered in returning to the tools and trying again. One thing that helps are of course what we call "hints," but these hints themselves only gain their relevance as we then see that we did not succeed and thus find ourselves looking for hints that we now have experiences of failure to use to make sense of the hints.

I realized when I was learning that I was not always tapping. It didn't seem all that necessary because the coffee was going to be pressed latter with the tamper. My instructor stood at my shoulder explaining that what is needed is either a sharp tap on the work surface or a tap on the side of the portafilter that rapidly evens out the dispensed coffee in the handle. Without an even spread of coffee, the pressurized hot water makes a channel for itself through the grains taking only a fraction of the flavorsome oils. The sharp tap for the beginner does not work though since it often just ends up knocking the coffee out of the portafilter or into a black snowdrift up against one side (Figure 7.1).

Seeing the uneven spread of the coffee, the instructor made me slow down what I was doing and make sure that I

Figure 7.1 Coffee grounds before they are tapped.
Source: Author.

Figure 7.2 A more balanced heap.
Source: Author

created a more balanced heap in the portafilter (Figure 7.2). When the balanced heap was tapped and then settled into the portafilter, it created already a mound that was centralized in the handle. When this mound was compressed then the resulting spread would be more even and less likely to channel the water through the coffee.

The experienced gaze of the barista takes in the problem—it is visible in the tilted heap of Figure 7.1. The lop-sided mound of grounds was then something I could also look out for, it becomes part of the way that one sees as a barista (Goodwin, 2000; Lynch, 2012). "Seeing as a barista" might still take us a distance from what is happening, the beginner uses the hint to scrutinize their mound of grounds and compares it to the other mounds around them and what they have been shown earlier, the expert inspects their mound, so fast and so routinely that it goes unnoticed (the momentary inspection that is). The visual inspection is part of the process of the making as it progresses in stages, each of which might need some form of repair. When I took the filter out from under the doser, I was then tapping the side of the portafilter rather than tapping it onto the work surface. As I looked around at the experienced baristas, I realized that they were, from time to time, also tapping the sides of their portafilters. Progress, I thought.

With one part of the trouble diagnosed, the coffee is still too variable. The other hint I am offered around where to concentrate my attention was on how to tamp the grounds down. Tamp too hard and the water flows too slowly through the granules taking too much out of them; too soft and the water rushes through barely extracting any flavors. The barista has to press the grounds again and again and again, making cup after cup of espresso, gradually finding just the pressure and angle of contact required with the tamper. To become a barista, you have to learn to tamp the same each and every time, to feel immediately when you tamped badly.[1]

The beginner barista tamps their coffee warily, tamps it slowly, inspecting the lie of the coffee after they have done so. As I watched our trainer and in later days as I watched my mentor in the café where I was put to work, and stole glances at other seasoned baristas at work; I noticed how some of them angle their shoulder to find that angle that will give them an even pressure. Some rotate the tamp while it is on the surface, though not all of them. I decide to rotate anyway reckoning it should provide a flatter surface and even out the pressure.

Color Judgments

Meantime at the training centre, our trainer keeps making espressos, we keep making espressos, and each time they are passed from hand to hand and he asks us "is it the right color?" We have been told that the crema[2] on top of the coffee should be "hazelnut." Even if we were all native speakers of English we might have difficulty pointing to a sample and saying "that is hazelnut." The nut, after all, comes in several different colors, its shell, its skin, the bare nut and these colors changes with age and cooking. However, if we consider the color "golden," which is often used to describe the crema on top of an espresso, we might begin to realize that it does not help trainees identify with precision when they have hit the right mark. Goodwin (1997) in describing how a group of lab chemists being trained to make a fiber that is referred to in the scientific literature as "jet-black" actually used "gorilla fur" as their descriptor and "orangutang hair" as the color indicating it was not quite right. Where "fur" helped highlight fibrousness so "hazelnut" help us trainees orient toward an uneven, spotty, or even stripey surface.

Our trainer does not show us the actual hazelnut but instead teaches us "hazelnut" by showing us sample after sample of the espresso crema drawn from the ones he makes and the ones we make. Some are too light, some too dark, and, thankfully, more and more are "hazelnut." We are hence working out this quite precise shade from its relation to these other shades of golden-brown. They are a color formed from tiny oily bubbles merging into streaks of dark brown and bright yellow. It is not quite right to say that it is one color, it is the texture and a combination of colors that is like those of hazelnuts. Our trainer shows us that the crema should have a duration too. He picks up cups of espresso that have been sitting for five minutes to show us that a good crema lasts a while. We are learning to see this [hazelnut][3] as its relational shade and in its temporal extension. As Goodwin (1997: 116) puts it, "what will count as valid instances of the color category is established within a public, socially constituted world of relevant activity, rather than in the mental processes of an isolated actor."

For the good barista, by using this [hazelnut] they are thus able to take a last check on their espresso as it travels in its small cup from machine to saucer. As our trainer makes us repeat as one more mantra: "no crema, no serva." Should we, having followed the steps, tamped as best we could, pressed the right button on the machine, still find that there is no crema on our espresso, we should throw it away and start again rather than serve it to a customer. There are some sceptical eyebrows raised over this, trainees already imagining the impossibility of doing this during a morning rush. However, the trainer reiterates the injunction, adding that, although it may seem like something that will annoy the customer, it will instead impress them because starting over shows you really care about the quality of their coffee. This provides him with an occasion to give us a little tip about the inferences that we can make about a customer from a certain kind of coffee being ordered. As he says, when a customer orders a ristretto[4] then this is someone who is serious about their coffee. Few customers will order it and we should think of it as a person at a bar ordering a 40-year-old single malt whiskey. Make sure you make it correctly, take your time, and definitely throw it away if it comes out bad.

We make several other possible coffees, different sizes in different cups, with chocolate, with shots of syrup, blended with ice to make iced coffees. In learning how to make a hot chocolate, our trainer amuses us by doing it in a flirty way, as if he were serving a woman who comes in every day and making it clear how he gives her extra big scoops of hot chocolate, while grinning and making small talk. He is making it clear that we can flirt, that we ought to flirt, that there can be more to this job than mirthlessly making drink after drink to a strictly controlled recipe. Where perhaps the best ristretto requires careful adherence to rules and recipes, the hot chocolate can only be gotten wrong by being measly with the chocolate. At another point, as we moved on to role playing, he played at being a customer who states flatly, as a challenge to all that a ristretto drinker holds dear: "I want an ordinary coffee." In return, we learnt how to offer an Americano with or without milk as a possible response to this challenging customer. We are hence being taught not just how to make the different kinds of drinks but also how those coffees, chocolates, and ice drinks related to kinds of customers, what those kinds of customers expect and how we should handle them.

From the Toolic to the Servic

Following the training has taken us quite naturally from a toolic world that is produced, after a reasonable amount of training, through the use of particular tools (e.g., the grinder, the tamper, and the espresso machine) to a world populated with the other half of the standardized relational pair of the barista—the customer. What is notable about a lot of the studies of skilled tool use is that they are not so much individualized since they are clearly about the socially available methods we have to use tools, it is that they are a little bit anti-social in the ordinary sense of this term. Conforming to the image of the craftsman (Sennett, 2008), these are the loners, dwelling in their quiet toolic places, the sheds, music rooms, and attic studies. If there is an intimacy, it is an intimacy with the games, DIY, puzzles, or other practices they are learning in and from. David Sudnow (1983) plays the computer Breakout for weeks and provides an insight into lived work of computer gameplay, toward the end of his book there's an artfully constructed chapter break where we suddenly surface from his small world of gameplay. We realize and remember he is a father spending hours playing the game out of time and place, while his son is in another room. There is an opponent in the "game" that Livingston (Livingston, 2008) is puzzling over yet this other member of society is restricted to their moves as part of the game. Early in ethnomethodology Garfinkel (1964) (Watson, 2009) studied games as well but he disrupted them and turned the attention of a player away from the game toward the multifarious courses of actions of the person that they are up against.

From the latter parts of the training described above, we are being brought around to the fact that the barista is from time to time working in a more Goffman-esque trade. Or, in fact, is working in hospitality and that that is the Goffman trade par excellence (excepting organized crime and the PR industry) given that his first study was of a hotel serving drinks and food to its guests (Goffman, 1956). It might indeed seem as if we are here in a setting like the restaurant where staff perform for customers and their success is measured by the cash left behind in tips (Crang, 1994). However, the order of service for the barista is distinct in that they serve at a counter (or bar) and the order and payment are dealt with as part of the same transaction.

What they do might be closer to the demeanor work of the bank teller (Harper, Randall, and Rouncefield, 2000) or responding to service requests in small shops of various kinds (Merritt, 1976; Moore, 2008). What is distinct to the café (and the restaurant) is that the product to be consumed is assembled in front of the customer and moreover the product is also usually consumed in the presence of its producer. A cup off coffee is, of course, also the end point of a much longer chain of production sites (Cowan, 2005; Liberman, 2011).

Customers as a Workplace Feature

After two days of having a trainer watching over you, and saying what happens next, you build up the expectation: your superior from the café tells you what to do. As you step behind the bar and really start becoming a barista in earnest, the small shock is that it is the customers that tell you what to do, or rather they make reasonable requests for drinks and food that you ought to be able to supply. They arrive at the counter and they say "two regular lattes please, one skinny," or "I'd like three regular cappuccinos, one with low fat milk, one large cappuccino, and a hot chocolate to take away, oh, no, actually can you make the large cappuccino a latte instead, ehm a large one too? heh heh." Sad to say there is no getting around this and the manageress, after asking me whether I could make coffee, then said "serve a customer." It's a fundamental shift. Not only do customers not ask you for the same drink each time (which would make your job nice and easy), they just keep coming. There is no time out for reflection, diagnosis or letting someone else have a go while you sit back down to laugh with your trainer at their efforts. They immerse you in the field of action with their orders.

Just learning how to get your beginner's hands on the decaff coffee, the herbal tea, the tongs for moving panini on the toaster and so on, takes repeated searching and reaching for the many things that are used to make customer orders. Your searching and reaching is cumbersome and halting, and sometimes it is done in plainly the wrong place as you search for a tea bag under the counter when it is on a high shelf. The experienced staff keep pointing out where things are to you, but you don't want to overstretch their patience. This frustrating inability to find the ingredients and equipment is combined with having to "walk through" each coffee recipe, saying to yourself "now what goes into a small mocha again?" and then asking someone else "what's in a small mocha?" And even while you are running over in your head the measures of coffee, the measures of chocolate, in what order you put them in: chocolate first or coffee first? You forget what other coffee the customer ordered. And you realize that you also forgot to ask them whether they wanted their coffees to take away or have-in. Smiling humbly you ask them "ehm I'm sorry, did you want your coffees to have in?" To your relief since you've already made coffee into mugs, they say "yes to have in."

At the outset, like most beginners, I was trying to make as few mistakes in making each coffee as possible, so I took it slow... and it's so slow. And it feels even slower to you as the barista than it does to the customer—this is the time that you experience where a minute of making a cappuccino stretches to feel like quarter of an hour and you are expecting the customer to be red in the face when you turn around, or to be halfway through writing a letter of complaint to your manager on the saucer that you laid out for them ages ago. Working alongside your maestro (as the café called your local mentor), they make each order so quickly. It seems possible that with enough practice you will reach the speed at which they make individual orders. What is more intimidating is that your maestro serves at least two customers whenever there is a queue, and I witnessed staff managing particularly long queues by taking on four orders at a time.

The customers arrive in little rushes that make you realize that you were in a quiet period previously, and as a beginner you have not yet registered what a quiet or a busy period really is, nor, entails (Laurier, 2008). After you have been through a rush then you have a little time for reflection and post hoc advice from the other baristas. Because making a cup of coffee or tea is an utterly familiar task for most people, it can be difficult to understand the different criteria around making them for customers for those who have not served at a bar or worked in a restaurant; customers are not like friends or family coming around to your place for a cup of tea who do not really mind if you have run out of Early Grey and give them Typhoo instead; friends, who appreciate the gesture and take what they are given with a smile and a thank-you. Customers want whatever it is you have listed as offering, and they want it to be the same as, or better than, the one they had last time.

Customers start to pace from foot to foot and mutter if they are waiting more than about two minutes to be served in a short queue (and they know the difference between a short queue where they should be served quick and a long queue at lunch when they will be served slowly). Customers, even without being unfriendly, can cause panic and fear for the beginner barista. Well they did for me, until I came to realize that most were forgiving. When I offered an apology for taking three times the time it took a normal member of staff, they would say things like: "don't worry you're just starting," "everybody has to learn sometime," or even "I think you're very brave." The experienced baristas differentiated between easy and "nightmare" customers (Manning, 2008), between regulars and the rest (Laurier, 2012). For me, on the first day, each customer seemed wildly unpredictable and hard to fathom. After a fortnight of serving customers I came to understand that the further fathoms of the customer was not my concern and that they shared an orientation to the order of service. So much so that, as (Kuroshima, 2010) notes, the abbreviations of requests and their fulfilment solidified our relationship.

As a barista you stand behind a bar, but the bar is so designed that there are no seats at the bar where customers can sit and expect to make small talk or tell their tragic life story to the bar staff. Nor are the customers becoming intoxicated with alcohol with all the tact that handling drunks requires of bar staff (Cavan, 1966). The barista has time-limited conversations with customers while they take their order, make their order up, and then dispense it while also dispensing with the customer. My trainer had told his trainees on numerous occasions that they should keep talking to the customer while making their order and try their best never to turn their backs on them. For the beginner barista who is still spelling out recipes, trying to recall orders, and trying not to press the wrong buttons on the machine, turning their back on the customer is pretty much inescapable and excusable for the time being.

From the Servic to the Logistic

Having considered the skills of tool use and then the production of order of service, there is still more to the barista's work, there is a practical reasoning and around the the flow of cutlery and crockery. This is part of what ethnomethodologists have described as the workflow from within (Bowers, Button, and Sharrock, 1995) though here turned toward the particulars of the café. Those studies like Goffman's the concentrated on the performance then tended to miss the props. Except that the cutlery and crockery are not "props," they do not have that loose relationship to purpose and function. They really must be clean, unchipped, and ready for use.

The cup's configuration as a workplace object for the barista's work is distinct from that of the customer and indeed for the many academics that have paused to contemplate the cup on their desk. The skills of the barista as part of the café staff turn upon the surveillance, monitoring, and flow the cups (and saucers and spoons and so on).

Doing the Dishes

In almost all cafés there are cups piled in rows according to size on top of the espresso machine. They run from the compact espresso cups to the capacious grande mugs, if the café goes that far and many of the third wave cafés have declined to supersize their coffee. One of the reasons the cups are there is because there is a heated plate keeping them constantly warm. An espresso is only a thimble measure of coffee and if you put it into a cold cup of solid ceramic then in less than a minute it will be cold as the ceramic it was trickled into.

The piles of warm cups are a shared resource for the baristas working behind the counter. Each of them draws their cups from this same store (although in high throughput cafés the machine is often mirror split to allow two teams on different cash tills to work from each side without crossing over and disrupting the other team's flow). The experienced staff working at speed, barely look to see where they are grabbing a regular cup from—they are sure that it will be there. They are sure that it will be prewarmed, clean, unchipped, and ready to be used. Their certainty is reliant on the baristas' steady and consistent replenishment of these rows of cups from the dishwasher, the ongoing rejection of dirty or chipped cups there. Working behind the counter I came to monitor the supply of cups like all the other baristas becoming aware of when it needed replenishment. Experienced staff were attuned to the rush hours and would do their best to make sure the machine was groaning with crockery beforehand, since there would be little or no time for collecting dirty cups, rinsing them, loading the dishwasher, waiting ten minutes, and then unloading and sorting it to the top of the machine.

At the busiest café, that I worked in the assistant manageress could often be heard to call out aloud that we needed more cups. All the working staff hearing this, and ones who were not engaged on an essential task, would start replenishing the cups. The assistant manageress also watched the display units of sandwiches, drinks, cakes, and pastries and would allocate staff to start replenishing or rearranging the units. In busy stores, like that one, replenishment and rearrangement is an urgent business as customers suck the water jugs dry, wolf down sandwiches at lunchtime, and make off with the choicest cakes. While senior café staff were in charge and ensured that restocking and tidying of display units occurred, all staff attended to them. I was taken at each store to be shown the importance of facing out sandwiches and cans.

It takes a leader and a team to keep the flow of crockery in circulation, making sure that it doesn't logjam at any point. The circulation has to be maintained even though supply and demand are temporally out of whack—at lunchtime everyone needs crockery but the supply is rapidly running out. Customers take about 20 minutes to finish before their crockery can be retrieved, and collecting the crockery takes time.

Rinsing the crockery of persistent lipstick and other magnetic gunk in the sink takes time, loading and unloading the dishwasher takes time, stacking the cups, plates and sorting the cutlery takes time, because it all has to be fitted inbetween the steps of the assembling of further drinks and food orders.

Concluding Thoughts

We have moved swiftly between the particular skills of making espresso that are the "whatness" of the barista. Without that capacity the person behind the counter is just another person behind the counter. That "what" of each and every job in the world remain an ongoing project for the descriptive enterprises of ethnomethodologists. As we have seen there is more to the "what" of becoming a barista than making coffee, it is a form of making a volatile and stimulating drink that is accomplished "while-u-wait." That phrase catching a collection of jobs where on requesting them to be done the customer can stand and watch them being done. Finally, these central parts of job are reliant upon the monitoring and movement of a workflow that refurnishes the cutlery, crockery, and comestibles for each next customer order.

What I have not been able to quite get in describing these early experiences of becoming a barista is how their cafés play part in the production and reproduction of communities (though see Laurier (2012) and Laurier and Philo (2006)). As I noted at the outset, Doug Harper's study of a small repair shop brings the mechanic's role in his rural area to the fore. It seems to me though that there was some surprise in realizing that such a figure might also be part of how community is replenished as their cars are repaired. Our expectation of the café is that it should help us, as Oldenburg (1999) put it, "get through the day." What we might overlook are the skills of the barista that underly the sociability.

Acknowledgments

The café people: Paul Ettinger, Lorraine Warwick, the store staff at Sheen, Long Acre, and Merrill Lynch, my fellow beginners and a grande grazie to Ignacio—"wild sociologist" and top trainer. Outside the café: Barry Brown, Julia Lossau, Nicky Burns, Hester Parr, Ludo, Sally, Derek, Erica, Euan, Catherine, Miles, and especially Karen.

Notes

1. Toolmakers for the coffee industry have tried to intervene here by building spring-loaded tamps that should then create the correct pressure on the grounds when pushed against them.
2. Crema is the layer of oily foam that sits on top of a cup of coffee, so called since it should be cream-like.
3. The square brackets are used by phenomenologists to turn around our *accepted* sense of a word and indicate that we will put our understanding on hold until we know what that thing properly consists of. The trainer, as a vernacular phenomenologist, takes his trainees on an investigation into seeing [hazelnut] – the correct shade, texture, and duration of the crema on top of the coffee.
4. A ristretto is an espresso type coffee with less water pushed through the grounds, thereby making a very short drink that carries only the first and arguably the best parts of the flavors and aromas of the beans.

References

Bjelić, D. I. (1995) An ethnomethodological clarification of Husserl's concepts of "regressive inquiry" and "Galilean physics" by means of discovering praxioms. *Human Studies*, 18(2), 189–225.

Bjelić, D. I. (2003) *Galileo's Pendulum: Science, Sexuality, and the Body-Instrument Link.* New York: State University of New York Pres.

Bowers, J., Button, G., and Sharrock, W. (1995) Workflow from within and without. Proceedings of the Fourth European Conference on Computer Supported Cooperative Work, 309–324.

Cavan, S. (1966) *The Liquor License: An Ethnography of Bar Behavior.* Chicago: Aldane.

Cowan, B. W. (2005). *The Social Life of Coffee.* New Haven [Conn.]: Yale University Press.

Crang, P. (1994). It's showtime: on the workplace geographies of display in a restaurant in southeast England. *Environment and Planning D: Society and Space*, 12, 675–704.

Dant, T. (2005) *Materiality And Society.* Maidenhead: Open University Press.

Faulkner, R. R. and Becker, H. S. (2009) *Do You Know –? The Jazz Repertoire in Action* London: University Of Chicago Press.
Garfinkel, H. (1964) Studies of the routine grounds of everyday activities. *Social Problems* 11, 225–250.
Garfinkel, H. and Rawls, A. W. (2002) *Ethnomethodology's Program.* London: Rowman & Littlefield Pub Incorporated.
Goffman, E. (1956) *The Presentation of Self in Everyday Life.* Edinburgh: University of Edinburgh.
Goodwin, C. (1997) The Blackness of Black: Color Categories as Situated Practice. In Resnick, L. B., Säljö, R., Pontecorvo, C., and Burge, B. (Eds) Discourse, Tools and Reasoning: Essays on Situated Cognition. New York: Springer, pp. 111–140.
Goodwin, C. (2000) Practices of Seeing, Visual Analysis: An Ethnomethodological Approach. In van Leeuwen, T. and Jewitt, C. (Eds) Handbook of Visual Analysis. London: Sage, pp. 157–182.
Harper, D. A. (1987) *Working Knowledge.* London: University Of Chicago Press.
Harper, R., Randall, D., and Rouncefield, M. (2000) *Organisational Change And Retail Finance.* London: Routledge.
Ingold, T. (2000) *The Perception of the Environment.* London: Routledge.
Kuroshima, S. (2010) Another look at the service encounter: progressivity, intersubjectivity, and trust in a Japanese sushi restaurant. *Journal of Pragmatics*, 42, 856–869.
Laurier, E. (2008) How breakfast happens in the cafe. *Time & Society*, 17(1), 119–134. DOI:10.1177/0961463X07086306.
Laurier, E. (2012) Encounters at the Counter: The Relationship between Regulars and Staff. In Tolmie, P. and Rouncefield, M. (Eds) Ethnomethodology at play. Farnham: Ashgate, pp. 179–198.
Laurier, E. and Philo, C. (2005) *The Cappuccino Community: Cafes and Civic Life in the Contemporary City (End of Award Report).* Glasgow: University of Glasgow and ESRC.
Laurier, E. and Philo, C. (2006) Cold shoulders and napkins handed: gestures of responsibility. *Transactions of the Institute of British Geographers.*
Liberman, K. (2013) *More Studies in Ethnomethodology, SUNY: New York.*
Livingston, E. (2008) *Ethnographies of Reason (Directions in Ethnomethodology and Conversation Analysis).* Aldershot: Ashgate.
Lynch, M. (1993) *Scientific Practice and Ordinary Action.* Cambridge: Cambridge University Press.
Lynch, M. (2013) Seeing Fish. In Tolmie, P. and Rouncefield, M. (Eds) Ashgate Publishing Company, (pp 287–308).

Manning, P. (2008). Barista rants about stupid customers at Starbucks: what imaginary conversations can teach us about real ones. *Language and Communication*, 28(2), 101–126. DOI:10.1016/j.langcom.2008.02.004.

Manzo, J. (2010) Coffee, connoisseurship, and an ethnomethodologically-informed sociology of taste. *Human Studies*, 1–15. DOI:10.1007/s10746-010-9159-4.

Merritt, M. (1976) On questions following questions in service encounters. *Language in Society*, 5(3), 315–357.

Moore, R. (2008) When names fail: referential practice in face-to-face service encounters. *Language in Society*, 37(03), 385–413.

Oldenburg, R. (1999) *The Great Good Place*. New York: Da Capo Press.

Ryle, G. (2009) *The Concept of Mind: 60th Anniversary Edition*. pp. 1–377.

Sennett, R. (2008) *The Craftsman*. London: Yale University Press.

Sudnow, D. (1983) *Pilgrim in the Microworld*. New York: Warner Books.

Watson, R. (2009) Constitutive practices and Garfinkel's notion of trust: revisited. *Journal of Classical Sociology*, 9(4), 475–499. DOI:10.1177/1468795X09344453.

8

COMMUNITY AND SOCIAL INTERACTION IN THE WIRELESS CITY: WI-FI USE IN PUBLIC AND SEMI-PUBLIC SPACES*

Keith N. Hampton and Neeti Gupta

Recent years have seen rapid growth in the availability of wireless broadband Internet access in public spaces. Providers and points of access take the form of municipal Wi-Fi networks (Muni Wi-Fi), such as those that have operated in Philadelphia and Toronto, community wireless networks, such as New York Wireless or Île Sans Fil in Montreal, advanced mobile phone networks (e.g., 3G), and Wi-Fi cafés, restaurants, bookstores, and related spaces (hereafter abbreviated as "Wi-Fi"). While there is a significant body of research addressing whether fixed Internet use increases, decreases, or supplements the ways in which people engage in residential (Hampton, 2007; Hampton and Wellman, 2003) and workplace settings (Quan-Haase and Wellman, 2006), few studies have addressed how the use of wireless broadband in public and semi-public spaces influences social life. Ubiquitous Wi-Fi adds a new dimension to the debate over how the Internet may influence the structure of community—the network of supportive ties that exist between individuals. It is unclear whether wireless Internet use in public spaces will facilitate greater engagement with people in public spaces or encourage a form of "public privatism." Will Wi-Fi use support public disengagement, with people withdrawing from the public realm in exchange for private spheres of influence, or will it facilitate new interactions and contribute to the development of a new public sphere? This chapter reports the findings of an exploratory study that examined how Wi-Fi was used and influenced social interactions in a series of Wi-Fi coffee shops. Observations were drawn from four different settings: paid and free Wi-Fi cafés in Boston and Seattle. The goal of this chapter is to provide an initial framework for understanding how Wi-Fi influences the interactions and structure of personal networks in a wireless city.

Privatism

In the past, the "wired" nature of desktop computing limited the potential for Internet use to blend into urban public spaces. With few exceptions, such as libraries, Internet cafés, and community technology centers, Internet use was confined to the home and workplace. The connection between Internet use and home-centeredness generated concern that new media use increased privatism (Graham and Marvin, 1996). Indeed, personal networks have become increasingly privatized, consisting of densely knit networks of interactions centered around the home, rather than diverse, loosely coupled interactions in more public settings. For example, a study of the size and composition of people's core "discussion networks" in 1985 and 2004 identified a shift from ties formed through voluntary associations, neighbors, and interactions in the public realm, toward networks increasingly dominated by kin and based around the home (McPherson, Smith-Lovin, and Brashears, 2006). While the authors of that study did not link Internet use directly with changes in the structure of social networks, it is notable that the time period observed by McPherson, Smith-Lovin, and Brashears (2006) corresponds with the rise of the "network society" (Castells, 1996). Their findings are consistent with observations of other home-based media, including television and the telephone, which have been linked to increased privatism (Putnam, 2000; Fischer, 1992).

The concern with privatism is the sacrifice of "bridging social capital" for "bonding social capital" (Putnam, 2000). Bonding social capital is formed through the interaction of tightly knit networks of similar others, often close friends and kin. Personal communities high in this form of social capital tend to provide generalized social support and to be high in reciprocity (Wellman and Wortley, 1990), but they can also be repressive and tend to be racially, culturally, behaviorally, and ideologically homogeneous (McPherson, Smith-Lovin, and Cook, 2001). Bridging social capital exists through access to diverse, and relatively "weak" social ties that provide specialized social support and access to novel information and resources (Burt, 1992; Granovetter, 1973). Individuals who have more bridging social capital, which can come only from participation in diverse social milieus, are more trusting, demonstrate greater social tolerance, cope with daily troubles and trauma more effectively, tend to be physically healthier (Cohen et al., 2000), and have access to more diverse information and resources, which has been shown to assist in search processes (such as finding a job; Granovetter, 1974).

The earliest evidence of the role Internet use plays in personal networks appeared to verify that the Internet amplifies the existing trend toward privatism. The work of Kraut et al. (1998) and Nie (2002) found that Internet use contributed to a decrease in the size of people's social circles, a reduction in public participation, and an increase in home centeredness. However, later research has found that the Internet does not significantly influence the allocation of day-to-day activities (Robinson et al., 2002), and supplements rather than replaces traditional modes of communication (Quan Haase et al., 2002). Those who use the Internet to communicate with their closest and most significant social ties are also in frequent contact in-person and through other media (Baym, Zhang, and Lin, 2004; Boase et al., 2006). Similarly, email users tend to have more social ties than non-users and email appears to be a particularly useful medium for maintaining contact with a larger number of relatively weak social ties (Zhao, 2006; Boase et al., 2006). Face-to-face and telephone contact remain the dominant modes of connectivity when people communicate with their closest ties (Boase et al., 2006). The general conclusion, that Internet use increases overall communication and possibly leads to larger networks, suggests that it is a possible counter force to privatism. However, the evidence on frequency of communication and network size alone, does not address directly the underlying concern of privatism, that networks are increasingly home-centered and homogeneous as a result of new media.

In an attempt to examine more closely the circumstances under which the Internet does or does not encourage privatism, a series of studies have examined the role Internet use plays in the formation and maintenance of neighborhood ties (Hampton and Wellman, 2003; Hampton, 2007). Early Internet adopters were found to have smaller neighborhood networks, but experience using the Internet was found to inoculate them from increased privatism. Over time, experienced Internet users increased the number of ties that they had from the parochial realm. The neighborhood networks of non-Internet users and those with less Internet experience lost ties over time, they become increasingly privatized (Hampton, 2007). These studies also found that the introduction of a neighborhood email list increased the number of weak social ties at the local level, and facilitated public participation (Hampton and Wellman, 2003; Mesch and Levanon, 2003; Hampton, 2007). The observation that Internet use affords both global and local connectivity, has been termed "glocalization" (Hampton, 2001). While these studies provide some promising evidence that home-based Internet use does not encourage privatism, and may even help reverse the trend, they are not conclusive, especially in light of the findings of McPherson, Smith-Lovin, and Brashears (2006). What is conclusive, is that the Internet has become integrated increasingly into everyday life (Haythornthwaite and Wellman, 2002).

The Public

With wireless Internet, for the first time it is possible to integrate intensive Internet use with the use of urban public space. Public spaces and public life play a unique role in the formation of social networks, opinions, and democracy. When referencing public space, urbanists typically refer to a "city's street, its parks, its places of public accommodation" such that "public space may be distinguished from private space in that access to the latter may be legally restricted" (Lofland, 1973: 19). Semi-public spaces, those spaces that are not completely "a world of strangers" (Lofland, 1973), nor domesticated, are recognized for the role that they play in public life (sometimes these spaces are termed the "parochial realm"). Habermas (1989) noted the role of such places, in the form of London coffeehouses and French salons, in the development of a public sphere for cultural and political debate. While Habermas (1989) argued that the growth of capitalism diminished the public sphere, Ray Oldenburg (1989) suggested that while such "third places" (differentiated from work and home) have declined, they continued to play an important role in the social life of Americans well into the twentieth century. Oldenburg (1989) noted that these semi-public spaces provide exposure to diverse social ties, they create a sense of place and community, and provide both serendipity and companionship.

As with the history of "community" (Hampton and Wellman, 2003; Wellman, 1999), the "public" has an extensive literature that documents its birth, transformation, death, and rebirth at the hands of societal (e.g., capitalism, industrialism, bureaucratization, etc.) and technological change (e.g., electricity, telephone, automobile, etc.) (Habermas, 1989; Sennett, 1977; Marvin, 1988; Fischer, 1992). The dominant interpretation of the relationship between public space and social interaction suggests that the modern urban environment is responsible for increasing social segregation, isolation, and noninvolvement. Public spaces are seen to afford bystander apathy (Latané and Darley, 1976), to generate stimulus overload (Milgram, 1970), and to be increasingly sanitized (Zukin, 1995; Hannigan, 1998). Yet, a considerable literature exists to suggest that street life is far from anonymous; it is full of symbolic interaction (Goffman, 1963; 1959; 1971), contains planned and fleeting encounters (Whyte, 1980; Coleman, 1962; Berkowitz, 1971; Lofland, 1973), it is a source of serendipity (Merton and Barber, 2004), and it is the setting for a range of informal interactions that contribute to social norms and public safety (Jacobs, 1961).

Public Privatism

It is unclear how wireless Internet access, which penetrates public spaces as the Internet already has penetrated private spaces, will influence the structure of people's networks and social interactions. If people use Wi-Fi in the same way as they use mobile phones, it is likely that Wi-Fi use will exasperate a trend toward "public privatism."

Mobile phones make community instantly accessible, social ties are reachable anywhere at any time; a form of community that Wellman et al. (2003) termed "networked individualism." Most people use mobile phones to call a small set of mostly strong ties (Ito and Okabe, 2006; Ling and Yttri, 2006). Email or texting (SMS) is used when voice communication is perceived to be inappropriate (Ito and Okabe, 2006), and to keep in touch with a larger more diverse set of contacts (Matsuda, 2005). Whether used for voice or SMS, mobile phones create a private sphere of interaction within public spaces. When people engage with their mobile phone, they create a private "cocoon" that reduces the likelihood of serendipitous public encounters (Harris, 2003), contradicts common expectations for public behavior (Ling, 2004), and diverts attention away from copresent others (including existing social ties) (Humphries, 2005). The mobile phone has made it less necessary to rely on anyone other than those who are already highly familiar; "those who have come into our sphere of friendship are always available" (Ling, 2000: 83). As argued by Goldberger (2003),

The great offense of the cell phone in public is not the intrusion of its ring, although that can be infuriating when it interrupts a tranquil moment. It is the fact that even when the phone does not ring at all, and is being used quietly and discretely, it renders a public place less public. It turns the boulevardier into a figure of privacy. And suddenly the meaning of the street as a public place has been hugely diminished.

The "public privatism" of interactions as a result of the mobile phone mirrors the findings from studies of how fixed Internet access has been used in semi-public spaces; "Private uses in Public Spaces" (Lee, 1999). The trend, of people socializing in small, intimate groups in private homes, rather than with large, diverse groups in public spaces, maybe augmented through the use of new mobile media by a tendency to socialize remotely with small, intimate groups in any space, at any time.

Ubiquitous Wi-Fi

Public spaces play a unique role in shaping and maintaining personal networks. Unlike the close, homogeneous, densely connected nature of social relationships that are likely to dominate private spaces (McPherson, Smith-Lovin, and Brashears, 2006; Putnam, 2000), of which the private home is the best example, public and semi-public spaces are more likely to be the setting for diverse social interactions. It is unclear how the penetration of the wireless Internet will influence interactions in these spaces or the broader structure of people's social networks. There may even be variation based on local culture, climate, the built environment, and how Wi-Fi is deployed (e.g., free vs. paid). At the most basic level, the growth of wireless Internet suggests two competing, although not mutually exclusive possibilities:

1. The ubiquitous availability of wireless Internet access will encourage greater participation in public spaces, lead to increased public interaction, and possibly diversify the composition of people's social networks; and

2. Public Wi-Fi use will consist of private cocoons of interaction that benefit existing close ties, distract from interactions with copresent others, and ultimately reinforce the existing trend toward privatism.

In the absence of Muni Wi-Fi projects that are fully operational and active for any extended period at the time of this research, to uncover initial evidence of how Wi-Fi use will influence the structure of community interaction, we rely on observations from those examples where Wi-Fi has already penetrated public and semi-public spaces, Wi-Fi coffee shops. Our observations of Wi-Fi use are exploratory; we did not attempt to test specific hypotheses in advance of our observations. Instead, based on what we observed of how Wi-Fi was used in coffee shops, we provide a first in-depth view of public Wi-Fi use, and sketch a theoretical framework for how interactions and networks may be augmented in the context of a ubiquitous wireless Internet.

Methods

We limited our observations to four Wi-Fi cafés in two cities, Seattle and Boston. One café in each city offered paid Wi-Fi, the other offered free access. Our selection of cafés was not random, all four of our cafés were familiar to at least one of the authors in advance of the study. However, neither of the authors was a regular at these coffeehouses. Gupta had previously lived and worked in Seattle and at the time of the study both Hampton and Gupta were residents of Cambridge, Massachusetts. Our cafés were selected to help control for variables that were exogenous to the influence of Wi-Fi. This included the potential for bias in our observations as a result of the culture of any one coffeehouse, the characteristics of surrounding neighborhoods, and the social qualities of different cities. We also recognized that the contrast between paid and free Wi-Fi might be a source of variation in users' experiences. Given the dominance of the Starbucks coffee chain (7,200 stores in 30 countries), its early adoption of Wi-Fi service (starting in 2001), and a deal with T-Mobile

(Deutsche Telekom) to offer paid Wi-Fi in the majority of its cafés, Starbucks seemed like a natural choice for our observations in order to maximize the generalizability of our findings. Given that the T-Mobile/Starbucks partnership was for paid Wi-Fi use, this necessitated that we select independent coffeehouses for our free Wi-Fi comparison.

We had initially hoped to observe Wi-Fi use in diverse urban environments, central business districts, and suburbs. However, after spending many hours in suburban coffeehouses we abandoned our plans after making very few observations of Wi-Fi use. Instead, we limited ourselves to commercial areas in or near the downtown core and the areas bordering the University of Washington and the Massachusetts Institute of Technology. We wanted to insure that the café's we selected were not unusual in a way that would raise questions as to whether our observations were as mundane as we hoped. For example, we initially wanted to make observations at Starbuck's first location, in Seattle's Pike Place Market, but it was quickly obvious that its role as a tourist destination made it atypical. In the end we spent time at eight different Seattle Starbuck's locations before we settled on the Starbucks at sixth and Union as a "typical" Starbucks setting; steady foot traffic, a small number of large, stuffed, comfortable purple chairs, and many less comfortable steal framed chairs with matching small tables. After a similar process, we selected a similarly pedestrian Starbucks located in Central Square (Cambridge; Greater Boston), between Harvard and the Massachusetts Institute of Technology.

It was surprisingly difficult to find completely free Wi-Fi café. Many had hidden price tags in the form of required purchases or time limits on use. Others advertised Wi-Fi but in practice served up such unreliable service that there were few takers. In Seattle we settled on Chaco Canyon Café (forty-seventh and Brooklyn near the University of Washington). The owner was a local community activist. The café offered an extensive selection of raw foods, organic juices, and fair trade coffees. The store had an "at home feeling" with ample tables made from golden oak. Wi-Fi access was installed and operated by the owner and his brother as an experiment to draw in new customers. In Boston we selected Trident Booksellers & Café (located on Newbury Street). Twenty years ago Trident's owner was an early pioneer of the bookstore-café combination that is now a standard configuration for the "big book" chains. The café has an open look with large windows that open to a trendy commercial street. The store provides Wi-Fi as part of NewburyOpen.Net, a free community Wi-Fi provider.

Our methods of observation were primarily qualitative. A total of 120 hours were spent in our four cafés between December 2003 and March 2004. A total of 30 hours were spent on direct observations in each café. Observations were made in two hour time blocks systematically distributed across hours of operation, roughly one third of the observations were made on weekends, the rest on weekdays.

Observations consisted of extended visits to each café with laptop in hand. The time in each coffeehouse was spent making detailed notes of how patrons with mobile devices interacted with each other and café staff. Careful notes documented each interaction, including the gender and approximate age of those involved, how the exchange was initiated, and the duration of the exchange. In addition to unobtrusive observations, we created a short web-based survey with questions on basic demographics, social networks, technology, and prior experiences in Wi-Fi cafés. As participants left the café, every fifth person who had used a laptop was given the web address to our online survey and a letter explaining the study. However, a low response rate lead us to abandon our survey. As it turned out, when we approached people with our survey, many of our participants spontaneously stopped to talk about their experiences. In total 20 unstructured exit interviews were completed, this represents about 8 percent of the total number of people we observed using laptops. Most interviews were conducted on the spot, when necessary they where scheduled for a later time, and on rare occasion they were completed through email correspondence.

Findings

The selection of four field sites was intended as a source of differentiation with the expectation that we would observe variation based on city, individual location, and free versus paid Wi-Fi services. However, our observations did not support even this simple expectation. We observed the most significant distinctions in social interactions based on different practices of Wi-Fi use. The settings we observed attracted users with two distinct activities. We present these practices as a typology with two ideal types: true mobiles and placemakers. It is important to recognize that while we present these activities as ideal types (Weber, 1946), there was some variation in the practices we observed, and we note such variation where appropriate.

True Mobiles

For "true mobiles," Wi-Fi coffee shops functioned as a backdrop for activities focused on the completion of "work" (studying, paid work, etc.). True mobiles identified the café as a "space of productivity." They would typically suggest that the store offered a change of setting that helped them to focus, or provided a source of creativity. One participant offered "It is nice to get out of the office, if I don't have a specific reason to be there. The change of pace seems to be good for my productivity." While another noted that "background noise helps me focus, and I know other people who think so too." The limited number of true mobiles that did not directly refer to the coffee shop as a productive space, told us that the café provided an "escape" that would in turn aid productivity when they returned to their place of work.

> I do a lot more writing at home, actually, but sitting in a coffeehouse is a temporary break. At home, this usually means that I walk a mile down to town, work there a while, and then walk back, so it's a matter of changing the dynamic. (Joey, male, 35, Boston Starbucks)

Early in our observations, our initial assumption was that semi-public spaces were not ideal for work productivity, and that the people we interviewed were offering a cover to justify "having no purpose" (Goffman, 1963: 58), possibly as an excuse for disengaging from a space that had a norm of social involvement, or as a reason for taking a break where there was a norm of work—possibly resulting from the presence of Wi-Fi. However, direct observations ultimately were inconsistent with our initial assumption, true mobiles were not providing a cover for disengagement, true mobiles were truly in the café with the sole purpose of work.

Whether a true mobile described their visit to the Wi-Fi café as an "escape" or a "space of productivity," there were no actual observable differences in their activities. All true mobiles spent their time almost completely engrossed in Wi-Fi and laptop use. Observations and interviews indicated that they were primarily engaged in sending email and surfing the web. Their laptops were not mere props, they were a means to a specific ends: productivity. Despite their own internal differentiation, there were no observable clues that those on an "escape" were immediately more or less "productive" in semi-public spaces than those specifically seeking efficiency.

True mobiles included all the "mobile workers" that we observed (those who were currently traveling "out of town" as part of their occupation), but did not specifically exclude those who did not travel or were not traveling currently for paid employment. True mobiles who were mobile workers often sought out Wi-Fi coffee shops to serve as primary, although temporary locations for employment activities. This contrasted with the majority of true mobiles that we observed, most true mobiles lived or work within a short distance of the cafés we studied. They tended to report a need to work from a fixed office location for most of their day, they used the café as a secondary, occasional extensions of local workplaces. It was not uncommon for true mobiles to report that they scheduled a specific day each week to spend at the café: "I work Monday to Thursday at the office and every Friday from Starbucks."

Locally based true mobiles identified with the Wi-Fi café as a space of productivity, but they were also likely to cite the coffeehouses as the location for another type of "escape"; an escape from the physical presence of their coworkers. This included home-based employees who by choice or other arrangement worked from home on specific days of the week, but sought the Wi-Fi café as a refuge from distractions at home—escape from a partner/spouse, children, and television. When compared to true mobiles of the more local variety, mobile workers differed only in whether they designated the Wi-Fi coffee shop as their primary workplaces, not in task: using Wi-Fi and their laptops to check email and surf the web.

As with most of the café customers that we observed, true mobiles participated in a minimal level of overt interaction with copresent others (both patrons and coffee shop employees). Much of their interaction was subtle and nonverbal. Their base level of engagement could be characterized by what Goffman called "civil inattention":

> One gives to another enough visual notice to demonstrate that one appreciates that the other is present (and admits openly to have seen him), while the next moment withdrawing one's attention from him so as to express that he does not constitute a target of special curiosity or design. (1963: 84).

The majority of true mobile's interactions were observed in the form of near constant keyboard use, and when interviewed, the communication they reported in the form of email and instant messages with colleagues, friends, and other existing members of their social network. The activities and interactions of the coffee shop were peripheral.

True mobiles both reported and were repeatedly observed avoiding the gaze of staff and other store inhabitants. Like the majority of other coffee shop patrons, true mobiles employed "portable involvement shields" (Goffman, 1966). Goffman described portable shields as fans, masks, and the use of people's hands to conceal facial expressions; used to shield oneself from others and to signal unavailability for more overt interactions. When seated at a table, the technology "have nots" used portable shields in the form of newspapers, magazines, and books, and the "haves"—true mobiles—used laptops. Cell phones were too small to make for good shields, but they did play a unique role for café patrons of all types. After ordering coffee at the counter, but before being seated and before coffee was poured, there was a particularly strong tendency for those with cell phones to use their mobile phones as a "legitimate momentary diversion" (Goffman, 1963: 59). Customers would take out their phone, stare at the screen, possibly move a dial or push a few buttons—presumably reviewing some content—but almost never initiated a new phone call. This was most frequent at our two Starbucks locations, where there was a norm that customers wait next to the counter for their coffee to be made before taking a seat.

In the use of involvement shields what differentiated true mobiles from other patrons was their persistence in their use of shields as barriers to interaction. Activities related to "work" were paramount, the extent that true mobiles could be distracted from these activities depended on the tempo and atmosphere in the café. When other patrons ignored the subtle (or not so subtle) signals of a shield and attempted to initiate verbal communication with a true mobile, they were unlikely to be met with eye contact, and were more likely to be met with no response (completely ignoring the other), or an abrupt 1–2 word retort, than what we observed when verbal contact was initiated with non-Wi-Fi users. For example, we observed one Wi-Fi user approach a true mobile at a neighboring table, he asked "Do you know how to get this working on my machine?" Without looking up, the true mobile replied, "No" and continued surfing the web. In another situation which was repeated often, a customer would enter a café and ask "Is this seat taken?" true mobiles were unlikely to do more than shake their heads, other patrons would make at least fleeting eye contact and provide a verbal response. When we pressed true mobiles about these encounters, they offered an explanation consistent with their attempt to remain focused on activities associated with work. At the same time, we would routinely observe the same true mobiles interacting with online contacts through email and instant messaging, although it was unclear from our advantage point if the exchanges were completely work related. The few times that true mobiles were observed in more extended unplanned in-person interactions were exchanges that involved meeting clients or other true mobiles. True mobiles who participated in extended copresent interactions were usually interacting with coworkers who arrived together, but on one occasion we did observe a true mobile talking to another patron who had the same new model of laptop.

Placemakers

In contrast with true mobiles, the primary activity of "placemakers" was "not to engage in paid work." They came to Wi-Fi coffee shops to "hang-out." The coffeehouse was not intended as a direct or indirect place of productivity. For the placemaker, the café was center stage, not peripheral. They were drawn by what one participant described as the "inherently casual sociability" of the physical setting. Placemakers used their laptops as a premise to enter and engage in the "social hubbub" of the space. This could mean direct copresent participation with existing members of their social network, unplanned encounters, or the pleasure Lofland (1998) ascribes to "public solitude" and "people watching." Like true mobiles, placemakers were observed regularly using wireless connectivity for email, web surfing, and instant messaging. However, the laptop was never their primary focus, the availability or potential for copresent sociability was their primary activity.

While placemakers were more likely than true mobiles to engage in unplanned interactions, placemakers were also more likely than true mobiles to enter a café alone. True mobiles occasionally arrived in pairs and settled in to complete some sort of "business," such as meeting with a client, but placemakers almost never arrived in pairs or larger groups.

A typical placemaker arrived alone, bought a coffee, and took a seat at a table for two next to a window. They would pull out their laptop, set it on the table, and become masters of the "momentary diversion" (Goffman, 1963). A great deal of time would be spent gazing out the window, looking around the café, adjusting personal belongings, slowly sipping coffee, searching for a power outlet, powering up, and then casually surfing the web and checking email, with prolonged intermittent pauses to glance around and outside the café.

In stark contrast to true mobiles, placemakers did not actively avoid the gaze of other patrons within the shared space. While placemakers participated in the rituals of civil inattention, a casual glance from another customer was more likely to be met with a fleeting smile than a quick look away. Once mutual awareness had been established, there was a higher probability that additional encounters would take place with a placemaker than with a true mobile. As one placemaker described his experience over the previous week:

> Met people face to face. Spoken to people several times. People ask me about laptops frequently, and about wireless services. Helped several people learn what they need to buy. Also, while in line about to order, meet people sometimes. Religious people sometimes use [the café] to make connections and invite me to their church. (Nancy, female, 28, Seattle Chaco Canyon)

While placemakers resembled true mobiles in their use of laptops and other devices as portable interaction shields, with true mobiles these same props were also the most likely observable sources for new interactions. For example, it was common if not routine for coffee shop patrons to glance at Wi-Fi users' computer screens. True mobiles typically would ignore such a glance or reposition their device to indicate unavailability; this behavior contrasted with placemakers who were less likely to signal unavailability. With surprising regularity, glances toward placemakers developed into discussions based on shared interest. We observed people engaged over products on an auction website, a site devoted to a local art show, and an online news site. This behavior also worked in reverse, Wi-Fi users were observed glancing at books and activities of other patrons, they engaged when there was shared affinity and on occasion used their laptops to find and share information. We witnessed serendipitous interactions that were as brief as a few seconds to those that extended more than 20 minutes. When interviewed, placemakers described many encounters of this nature, as often with coffee shop employees as with customers.

Overall, the total number of observed conversations between previously unknown customers was small, in each hour maybe a couple of interactions that were more than the most fleeting; requesting a chair, moving a bag, passing a condiment. However, more serendipitous verbal interactions were recorded between placemakers and other patrons than between patrons in general. When interviewed, almost 50 percent of placemakers reported meeting someone new at a Wi-Fi café, very few true mobiles reported an unscheduled meeting. When true mobiles did report a serendipitous encounter, they tended to be instrumental, such as a commonly observed exchange associated with negotiating access to a power plug for a laptop, and they were more fleeting, such as a glance or small gesture exchanged with other "Wi-Fi regulars" –which we observed most frequently with a group of true mobiles who shared a morning routine: Starbucks, email, a latte, and a smile.

While placemakers almost always arrived alone, and more often than not left alone, both placemakers and true mobiles experienced scheduled and unplanned encounters with existing social ties. About a third of placemakers, but only a small fraction of true mobiles would be met by an acquaintance at some point. In all the situations, we observed the arriving party would not engage in their own private Wi-Fi use. Instead, the laptop was likely to become a shared focus of attention. For example, one person would read off the screen to another, or two people would watch a video together.

Unlike true mobiles, it was unusual to find a placemaker who was not local. Placemakers were almost always regular customers at the same café and they lived or worked in close proximity. Placemakers were more frequent visitors to Wi-Fi cafés than true mobiles. Most true mobiles reported 1–2 visits per week, placemakers visited almost daily. All Wi-Fi users spent in excess of 30 minutes in the coffee shop on a single visit, and three in ten stayed more than 4–5 hours.

While our observations were of a continuum that ranged from true mobiles to placemakers, not an absolute dichotomy, for the most part the distinctions were obvious, users did not move back and forth between types within the same setting. Placemakers did not immerse themselves in shielded, private cocoons of interaction with the goal of completing work. Placemakers were open if not actively interested in communicating with colocated others, it was their primary ativity.

Conclusion

The Future of Community

In our observations of the semi-public space offered by Wi-Fi cafés, we found contrasting uses for wireless Internet and competing implications for community. Two types of practices, typified in the behaviors of "true mobiles" and "placemakers," offer divergent futures for how the deployment of ubiquities Wi-Fi may influence the structure of social networks and social relationships in public spaces.

A shift in Internet use away from the home and workplace and into the semi-public environment of a café is by definition a shift away from privatism. True mobiles advanced this trend in their use of Wi-Fi spaces as an "escape," but in this case the substitution of private for public space did not address the underlying implications of privatism. While true mobiles escaped the confines of private space, they did not embrace new opportunities for public interaction, at least not unplanned, serendipitous encounters with copresent others. Instead, true mobiles actively resisted the public, they attempted to erect barriers, physically in the form of interaction shields, and sociologically through their avoidance of gaze and verbal contact. True mobiles used public space for very private activities, those they associated with the productivity of work, and likely for computer-mediated maintenance of their existing social network. As with mobile phone users, true mobiles embraced wireless connectivity for "public privatism." True mobiles used wireless Internet access to help them transform the network structure of work and community to enable connections to people-in-any-place rather than to people-in-place; "networked individualism" (Wellman et al., 2003). In addition, the true mobiles who also spent part of their time doing paid work from home consciously used Wi-Fi-enabled spaces as an escape from home-based ties –(partner and children). It is not clear if this escape from the nuclear family is a reaction to home centric personal networks, an escape from the psychological overload of intensive kinship relations, or an additional trend toward individualism and social isolation that has the potential to narrow further the size and composition of social networks.

In contrast to true mobiles, placemakers embraced the wireless Internet precisely for its ability to connect to the activities afforded by public space. The primary activity of placemakers was "not work," it was: interactions with copresent social ties, serendipitous exchanges, and availability for interactions with strangers. Placemakers used the public setting of wireless Internet connectivity as a means for local, place-based interactions, what Hampton and Wellman (2003) have previously referred to as "glocalization." This is not to say that placemakers did not use the environment of Wi-Fi cafés to maintain their existing networks, as with true mobiles many of their Wi-Fi-enabled activities were likely to be computer-mediated exchanges with established social ties, but consistent with the traditional activities of coffee shops, placemakers also had many planned and unplanned face-to-face encounters. What fundamentally differentiated placemakers from true mobiles was their use of public space for interactions that were not private.

"Community" is not a normative concept. It is the structure of supportive relations that exists between individuals. Large-scale social change can affect how individuals structure their networks, and in turn constrain behavior, influence how information is channeled, and affect the allocation of resources. The underlying question that this chapter attempts to address is whether or not the introduction of ubiquitous wireless Internet connectivity into the urban environment will alter the prevailing trend in how personal networks are structured: the tendency toward privatism. The answer is that it is too early to tell, but there are signs leading in divergent directions.

Networked individualism and glocalization are parallel paths, each involves a transformation to the structure of community that is a result of the affordances of the Internet. It is possible that the tendency toward networked individualism or glocalization will vary by individual, and possibly vary for that individual at different stages in the life cycle (Hampton, 2007), but it is not only a matter of personal choice. In a situation where the activities of "public privatism" dominate within even a marginal segment of public spaces, a "neighborhood" or "contextual" effect may be the result. Neighborhood effects are used to explain the role of community level characteristics in social tie formation in the context of neighborhood communities (Sampson, Morenoff, and Gannon-Rowley, 2002). Specifically, individuals who are highly motivated to form social ties, but who live in a neighborhood where few others are available or interested in forming relationships, are structurally disadvantaged relative to similarly motivated (or even lesser motivated persons) in a neighborhood where people are open to tie formation. The network constraints are very different. The same effect applies to the likelihood of serendipity and other encounters in public spaces; it takes at least two for interaction and if no one else is interested or available ultimately you will remain alone. The higher the number of people engrossed in public privatism within any space, the less opportunity for new tie formation.

The Future of Wireless Internet in Urban Public Spaces

The deployment of wireless Internet use in public spaces will initiate a path dependence that ultimately will lead to the domination of either a new public privatism, or increased public participation that will help to counter the existing trend of privatism. However, Wi-Fi is not in and of itself deterministic, but decisions related to the deployment of the technology afford different types of social interactions. Although we have not stated it until now, it is true that we found more true mobiles in our paid Wi-Fi Starbucks locations, and a greater number of placemakers where free Wi-Fi could be found. However, we did not observe a simple one-to-one relationship, where the presence of free Wi-Fi simply created public interactions. The environment of paid Wi-Fi was simply more conducive to the activities of true mobiles and less so to placemakers. As one participant described,

> [People] go to Starbucks because people don't want to experiment with their coffee. They usually like to get coffee they like, and Starbucks promises them exactly that. Similarly, people who are looking for Wi-Fi connections will go to places where they know they will get a good connection, and where they can sit for some time and work. (Sandy, male, 35, Seattle Chaco Canyon Café).

Even in those environments that were more favorable to placemakers, coffeehouses often adjusted their environment to limit their presence. Free Wi-Fi cafés employed strategies to discourage people from gathering or feeling overly welcome. For example, when interviewing at Trident Café we learned that management had recently removed all power outlets from customer areas. While visiting other free cafés, we observed that this was a common practice, along with actively limiting Wi-Fi access during peak hours, reducing table space, and established rules controlling access to toilet facilities. Employees would use the guise of customer service to ask patrons if they needed anything, but when we questioned, many admitted that it was a strategy to encourage "wireless squatters" to buy something or leave. The perception of free Wi-Fi providers was that their customers had a tendency to loiter and stay around socializing for long periods of time, taking space away from "legitimate" customers. Even in situations where Wi-Fi cafés had the potential to afford the broad community interactions of a "third place" (Oldenburg, 1989), private control over semi-public spaces actively worked to reduce the potential for wireless Internet to afford social interactions.

As access to a ubiquitous wireless Internet Wi-Fi blossoms, it is reasonable to assume that the strategies employed by the owners of semi-public spaces to limit the activities of true mobiles will be carried over by governments and private organizations (such as business improvement districts and Internet service providers) in their attempt to regulate public spaces to make them most welcoming to paying consumers. Yet, commercial interests that drive away placemakers may find themselves driving away the majority of public Wi-Fi uses. Even true mobiles are drawn to public Wi-Fi by the social characteristics of the setting, and as William Whyte (1980) noted in *The Social Life of Small Urban Spaces*, what attracts people the most is other people. As cities deploy Muni Wi-Fi—whether purely public initiatives, partnerships with private service providers, or driven solely by private investment—if public spaces are to support diverse opportunities for social interaction, and the benefits to democracy and public safety that such interactions afford, local governments must reevaluate existing policy on the access and design of public space. Conventional considerations related to the design of public space to maximize for social uses (Whyte, 1980) must be reconsidered in light of the unique requirements of new media use, such as the provision of power outlets, flat surfaces for laptops, and shade to view digital displays. It is also important to encourage additional research on Wi-Fi use, in public settings like parks and plazas. Observations of these spaces will help us to understand how the built environment can be used to help Wi-Fi users balance privacy, mutual surveillance, public safety, the opportunity for serendipitous encounters, and other social behaviors. In addition, observation of Wi-Fi use must be coupled with longitudinal studies of wireless users to clarify what ethnographic studies are unlikely to be able to examine, the extent to which the networks of placemakers and true mobiles are otherwise home centered, the overall diversity of their social ties, and whether they are actually exchanging time that otherwise would have been spent in the sanctity of the private space for a new public life.

Acknowledgments

We would like to thank the Department of Urban Studies and Planning, and the Comparative Media Studies Program at the Massachusetts Institute of Technology. This manuscript benefited from the comments of Pablo Boczkowski, Henry Jenkins, Marc Smith, Barry Wellman, and the editors and anonymous reviewers of *New Media & Society*. We would also like to thank the anonymous reviewers of the *2007 International Conference on Communities and Technologies*, where a preliminary version of this paper was presented. Direct correspondence to Keith Hampton (keith.hampton@rutgers.edu). For more papers related to this work, visit http://www.mysocialnetwork.net.

Note

*This article first appeared in New Media & Society, 10(6), December/2008. All rights reserved. ©SAGE Publications Ltd, 2008.

References

Baym, N., Zhang, Y. B., and Lin, M.-C. (2004) Social interactions across media: interpersonal communication on the internet, telephone and face-to-face. *New Media & Society*, 6, 3, 299–318.

Berkowitz, S. D. (1971) A cross-national comparison of some social patterns of urban pedestrians. *Journal of Cross-Cultural Psychology*, 2, 129–144.

Boase, J., et al. (2006) *The Strength of Internet Ties*. Washington, DC: Pew Internet & American Life Project.

Burt, R. (1992) *Structural Holes*. Chicago: University of Chicago Press.

Castells, M. (1996) *The Rise of the Network Society*. Oxford: Blackwell.

Cohen, S., et al. (2000) Social integration and health: the case of the common cold. *Journal of Social Structure*, 1, 3, 1–7.

Coleman, J. S. (1962) Comment on Harrison White, 'chance models of systems of casual groups.' *Sociometry*. 25, 172–176.

Fischer, C. (1992) *America Calling: A Social History of the Telephone to 1940*. Berkeley: University of California Press.

Goffman, E. (1959) *The Presentation of Self in Everyday Life*. London: Penguin.

Goffman, E. (1963) *Behavior in Public Places: Notes on the Social Order of Gatherings.* New York: Free Press.
Goffman, E. (1966) *Behavior in Public Places.* Free Press.
Goffman, E. (1971) *Relations in Public: Micro-Studies of the Public Order.* New York: Basic Books.
Goldberger, P. (2003) Disconnected urbanism: the cell phone has changed our sense of place more than faxes, computers, and e-mail. *Metropolis Magazine,* http://www.metropolismag.com/cda/story.php?artid=254, accessed March 27, 2007.
Graham, S. and Marvin, S. (1996) *Telecommunications and the City: Electronic Spaces, Urban Places.* London: Routledge.
Granovetter, M. (1973) The strength of weak ties. *American Journal of Sociology,* 78, 6, 1360–1380.
Granovetter, M. (1974) *Getting a Job.* Cambridge, MA: Harvard University Press.
Habermas, J. (1989) *The Structural Transformation of the Public Sphere.* Cambridge, MA: MIT Press.
Hampton, K. (2001) *Living the Wired Life in the Wired Suburb: Netville, Glocalization and Civic Society,* PhD dissertation, Department of Sociology, University of Toronto.
Hampton, K. (2007) Neighborhoods in the network society: the e-neighbors study. *Information, Communication and Society,* 10, 5.
Hampton, K. and Wellman, B. (2003) Neighboring in Netville: how the internet supports community and social capital in a wired suburb. *City and Community,* 2, 3, 277–311.
Hannigan, J. (1998) *Fantasy City: Pleasure and Profit in the Postmodern Metropolis.* New York: Routledge.
Harris, K. (2003) Keep your distance: remote connection. *Journal of Community Work and Development,* 4.
Haythornthwaite, C. and Wellman, B. (2002) The Internet in Everyday Life: An Introduction. In Wellman, B. and Haythornthwaite, C. (Eds) The Internet in Everyday Life. Oxford: Blackwell, pp. 3–44.
Humphries, L. (2005) Cellphones in public: social interactions in a wireless era. *New Media & Society,* 7, 6, 810–833.
Ito, M. and Okabe, D. (2006) Intimate Connections. In Kraut, R., Brynin, M. and Keisler, S. (Eds) Computers, Phones, and the Internet: Domesticating Information Technology. New York: Oxford University Press, pp. 235–247.
Jacobs, J. (1961) *The Death and Life of Great American Cities.* New York: Random House.
Kraut, R., et al. (2002) Internet paradox revisited. *Journal of Social Issues,* 58, 1, 49–74.

Kraut, R., et al. (1998) Internet paradox: a social technology that reduces social involvement and psychological well-being? *American Psychologist*, 53, 9, 1017–1031.
Latané, B. and Darley, J. (1976) *Help in a Crisis: Bystander Response to an Emergency*. Morristown, NJ: General Learning Press.
Lee, S. (1999) Private uses in public spaces: a study of internet café. *New Media & Society*, 1, 3, 331–350.
Ling, R. (2000) Direct and Mediated Interaction in the Maintenance of Social Relationships. In Sloane, A. and van Rijn, F. (Eds) Home Informatics and Telematics: Information, Technology and Society. Boston: Kluwer, pp. 61–86.
Ling, R. (2004) *The Mobile Connection*. San Francisco, CA:Morgan Kaufmann.
Ling, R. and Yttri, B. (2006) Control, Emancipation, and Status. In Kraut, R., Brynin, M., and Keisler, S. (Eds) Computers, Phones, and the Internet: Domesticating Information Technology. New York: Oxford University press, pp. 219–234.
Lofland, L. (1973) *A World of Strangers*. New York: Basic.
Lofland, L. H. (1998) *The Public Realm: Exploring the City's Quintessential Social Territory*. New York: Aldine de Gruyter.
Marvin, C. (1988) *When Old Technologies Were New: Thinking about Electric Communication in the Late Nineteenth Century*. New York: Oxford University Press.
Matsuda, M. (2005) Mobile Communications and Selective Sociality. In Ito, M., Okabe, M. and Matsuda, M. (Eds) Personal, Portable, Pedestrian: Mobile Phones in Japanese Life. Cambridge, MA: MIT press, 123–142.
McPherson, M., Smith-Lovin, L., and Brashears, M. E. (2006) Social isolation in america: changes in core discussion networks over two decades. *American Sociological Review*, 71, 3, 353–375.
McPherson, M., Smith-Lovin, L., and Cook, J. M. (2001) Birds of a feather: homophily in social networks. *Annual Review of Sociology*, 27, 415–444.
Merton, R. K. and Barber, E. (2004) *The Travels and Adventures of Serendipity: A Study in Sociological Semantics and the Sociology of Science*. Princeton, NJ: Princeton University Press.
Mesch, G. S. and Levanon, Y. (2003) Community networking and locally-based social ties in two suburban localities. *City & Community*, 2, 4, 335–351.
Milgram, S. (1970) The Experience of living in cities. *Science*, March, viewed.
Nie, N., Hillygus, S., and Erbring, L. (2002) Internet Use, Interpersonal Relations and Sociability: A Time Diary Study. In Wellman, B. and

Haythornthwaite, C. (Eds) *The Internet in Everyday Life*. Oxford: Blackwell, pp. 215–243.

Oldenburg, R. (1989) *The Great Good Place: Cafes, Coffee Shops, Community Centers, Beauty Parlors, General Stores, Bars, Hangout, and How They Get You Through the Day*. New York: Paragon House.

Putnam, R. (2000) *Bowling Alone*. New York: Simon & Schuster.

Quan-Haase, A. and Wellman, B. (2006) Hyperconnected Net Work. In Heckscher, C. and Adler, P. (Eds) The Firm as a Collaborative Community: Reconstructing Trust in the Knowledge Economy. New York: Oxford University Press, pp. 281–333.

Quan Haase, A., et al. (2002) Internet, Social Capital, and Information Seeking. In Wellman, B. and Haythornthwaite, C. (Eds) The Internet in Everyday Life. Oxford: Blackwell, pp. 291–324.

Robinson, J. P., et al. (2002) The Internet and Other Uses of Time. In Wellman, B. and Haythornthwaite, C. (Eds) *The Internet in Everyday Life*. Oxford: Blackwell, pp. 244–262.

Sampson, R., Morenoff, J., and Gannon-Rowley, T. (2002) Assessing "neighborhood effects": social processes and new directions in research. *Annual Review of Sociology*, 28, 443–478.

Sennett, R. (1977) *The Fall of Public Man*. New York: Knopf.

Weber, M. (1946) *From Max Weber: Essays in Sociology*. New York: Oxford University Press.

Wellman, B. (1999) The Network Community: An Introduction. In Wellman, B. (Ed.) Networks in the Global Village. Boulder, CO: Westview, pp. 1–47.

Wellman, B., et al. (2003) The social affordances of the internet for networked individualism. *Journal of Computer-Mediated Communication*, 8, 3.

Wellman, B. and Wortley, S. (1990) Different strokes from different folks: community ties and social support. *American Journal of Sociology*, 96, 558–88.

Whyte, W. H. (1980) The Social Life of Small Urban Spaces. Washington, DC: Conservation Foundation.

Zhao, S. (2006) Do internet users have more social ties? A call for differentiated analyses of internet use. *Journal of Computer Mediated Communication*, 11, 3, pp. article 8.

Zukin, S. (1995) *The Cultures of Cities*. Cambridge, MA: Blackwell Publishers.

9

DESIGN FOR SOLITUDE

Erling Dokk Holm

In the fields of urban sociology, urbanism, and urban geography, there has been a growing interest in the social aspects of urban life. Several studies have explored the potential for creating social capital in urban contexts. The sociologist Ray Oldenburg contributed to this field of study with his book *The Great Good Place: Cafes, Coffee Shops, Community Centers, Beauty Parlors, General Stores, Bars, Hangouts, and How They Get You Through the Day* (1989); the book emphasizes the longing for community, friendships, and a common locality. Oldenburg also coined the term, "third place," which has become immensely popular and has even been adopted on a huge scale by commercial operators in the service sector, such as Starbucks. He notes that modernist urban planning, extensive use of cars and large-scale shopping concepts have destroyed the traditional urbanism. His reflections coincide with Jane Jacob's views in her legendary book, *The Death and Life of Great American Cities* (1961). *In Bowling Alone: The Collapse and Revival of American Community* (2000), the political scientist Robert Putnam sheds light on the dramatic fall in community participation in the United States; among other things, he comments on the demise of the classical North American urban lifestyle, strongly related to the growth in suburbanization and shopping malls. In their book, *In Search of New Public Domain* (2002), the Dutch urbanists Marten Hejer and Arnold Reijndorp also write about social urban spaces, where people meet and establish contact.

Several of the most empirical-based studies published in this field of research have focused on libraries and their function as public spaces. The idea that the public library is some sort of new and open space where people can interact and establish ties—weak and strong—and thereby also build social capital, seems to find strong support in many of these studies (see, for instance, Audunson et al., 2007). This chapter focuses on the above topics of research in relation to the empirical study of coffee bars mentioned above; and even if there are many customers in coffee bars who engage in conversations with strangers, make friends, and build social structures, the majority of customers come, sit, and leave on their own. This chapter investigates why so many come on their own, and why this group seems to be so dominant in the coffee bars examined.

The chapter is based on empirical material collected between October 2008 and June 2010. The data consists of qualitative data (observations, drawings, photographs, and interviews) and quantitative data (statistical data) from three different coffee bars in Oslo, Norway. These data sets form the empirical base for my PhD thesis, *Coffee and the City. Towards a Soft Urbanity* (Holm, 2010).

The three coffee bars investigated in the above thesis have a diverse clientele, and are located in rather different environments. *Evita* is located in a traditional working class area, the central Eastern part of Oslo, which is inhabited and frequented by the working class people as well as more recent non-Western immigrants. The customers and location of the latter contrasts with *Java* and *Kaffebrenneriet*, which are in a central part of the city.

The Western hemisphere has seen a long and consistent increase in the number of coffee bars and consumption of the so-called speciality coffee. Since the mid-1980s, when the Seattle-based company Starbucks started to spread across the United States, a major shift in the urban consumption of coffee can be observed. In these bars, espresso-based coffee is sold through establishments that are easily identified through their visual character. In other words, coffee bars are distinctly different from "cafés," although the distinction between the two is sometimes blurred. In many small, medium-sized, and large cities in the developed world, and also in many less-developed regions, the increase has become visually apparent. Oslo, the capital of Norway, where the empirical material for this chapter was collected, is perhaps a typical example. The city saw extremely rapid growth in coffee bars during the late 1990s: the central parts of the city had no coffee bars in 1994, while ten years later the number was close to 100.

This chapter examines the question how the design of coffee bars relates to the use and the users of coffee bars.

First: What Is a Coffee Bar?

From my work on coffee bars I have concluded that a coffee bar may be identified through the structure of the sale and through its design. In characterizing a coffee bar, the figures speak for themselves: 75–90 percent of a coffee bar's revenue may be traced back to the sale of coffee drinks. Although a coffee bar may sell Danish pastries, croissants and the like, other beverages, as well as ground coffee and coffee beans, the single major product sold is the coffee drink. Compared to restaurants and cafés, this sales structure reveals a specific distinction—in other words, coffee bars may be defined by their sales figures relating to the products sold.

The design of coffee bars is the other distinct feature. Most coffee bars may be identified through a set of design parameters. The smallest ones have a central counter and counters at the windows, and possibly a free-standing bar somewhere else in the bar. The larger coffee bars often also have a set of tables and in some cases a few sofas and larger chairs.

Central to the design of the coffee bar is the counter where the customers line up, where the coffee drinks are produced and where the transaction between barista and customer takes place. This physical layout is remarkably similar in most coffee bars. The main counter is often long, seldom short – generally between two and four meters – and it is usually equipped with an espresso machine.

Most window bar-counters are between 30 and 50 cm deep, providing enough space for a cup of coffee, a plate with a baguette and a newspaper. The window bar-counters are always designed for use with bar stools and are typically 1.30 meters high.

The main counter is often described as "the heart of the coffee bar," an apt description given the centrality of sales of coffee from the bar. With the espresso machine placed on the counter, the baristas are able to communicate with the customers as they operate the machine. Through this feature, they are thus "connected" to the customers through the whole process from ordering to producing/serving to payment. The baristas operate the espresso machine and also sell other supporting products such as croissants and sandwiches. These products are also usually reachable from the counter, as most of them are placed in a cooled case underneath the counter.

An important function supported by the main counter is the intimate relation a coffee bar offers its users. The coffee bar's customers line up in front of the counter, and are quickly served. In most cases—at least in most of the coffee bars I have visited—a customer will generally be served by a barista in three minutes or less. Of course, there may be times when it takes longer, but in my empirical material they were few, representing less than one per cent.

The majority of customers have regular habits. They often order the same items every time they visit a coffee bar; and in many coffee bars a large part of the clientele are what the baristas call regulars. In some of the coffee bars, I have studied more than seven out of ten are regulars; this phenomenon may explain why baristas are able to serve a line of customers so quickly. When a trained barista observes a regular customer, the speed of the queue will be optimized. An efficient barista is characterized by his or her ability to spot regular customers in the queue, and start preparing their beverages in advance. In smaller coffee bars, one barista often does all the operations, operating the till and preparing and serving the coffee. However, in most coffee bars, the baristas alternate roles. Often one will be in charge of making and serving the coffee, while another operates the till and takes the food and coffee orders.

Figure 9.1   The coffee bar, *Kaffebrenneriet.* Illustration: Kyrre Holmeseth.

The queue is also a social line of people, as illuminated by Figure 9.1. They chat, at least some of them always do, either with other people in the queue or with the men and women behind the counter. The queue is a connection between the different elements in the coffee bar, and its most vital and social sphere.

After having ordered the coffee, in most coffee bars the customer will move further down the counter and pick up the coffee at the end of the counter once it is ready. If the coffee ordered is not a "take-away," the customer will then in most cases find a place to sit. In a normal coffee bar, there will be counters or bars along the windows, maybe a freestanding bar somewhere else in the locale, and perhaps small tables where one can sit in regular chairs. As the drawings illustrate—see, for instance, Figure 9.1—the bars along the windows will in most cases count for a substantial part of the coffee bar's capacity, and in many of them represent the majority of "seating."

Second: How Is the Coffee Bar Used?

The three coffee bars investigated here have a diverse clientele and are located in rather different environments. Evita is located in the traditional central Eastern part of Oslo, an area that reflects the structural changes that have recently taken place in Norwegian society, representing a mix of traditional white working class, non-Western immigrants, and the new gentrified middle class. Evita is a coffee bar with a diverse blend of social and cultural segments, and stands out in comparison to many of other coffee bars in the neighborhood that have a more uniform clientele.

As mentioned earlier, Java and Kaffebrenneriet are located in a central part of town characterized by a much more homogeneous neighborhood in a more well-to-do area, largely populated by a white well-educated upper middle class. However, the two different coffee bars seem to be identified with two different segments of this population. Kaffebrenneriet has more female customers; the average customer is a little older than at the other coffee bar, and women employed in the public sector constitute the single largest customer group. Kaffebrenneriet is also part of a chain of coffee bars, in contrast to Java, which is a "connoisseur" type of coffee bar. At Java the level of dedication and refinement is higher, which might explain why the customers here tend to find their employment in the so-called creative businesses, and a majority of them are employed in the private sector.

There are also two striking similarities between the three coffee bars: the age groups and the fact customers arriving on their own constitute the largest group (seven out of ten). The coffee bars rarely attract customers over 60, and few are younger than 20.

These two features differentiate coffee bars from cafés and restaurants. Although I have not used the same thorough observations and statistical methods concerning restaurants and cafés, I have produced brief statistics for three parallel cafés/restaurants to demonstrate the differences. In these three businesses, the percentage of customers arriving on their own is normally less than one out of ten. Most come in groups of two, but also larger groups; families often arrive together. In these three places, elderly people are an integrated part of the clientele, even if they do not dominate the customer base.

Third: Why Do They Arrive on Their Own, and Sit and Leave on Their Own?

In the interviews I conducted with many of the users, a set of varied explanations emerged. When users elaborated on their use different groups could be identified. One group I term the "instrumentalists"; they used the coffee bar for instrumental reasons, for instance, as a break in their workday. One person I interviewed used his coffee bar as a space where he would seek "refuge" when the burdens of work became too much, especially with regard to work-related social commitments such as lunch with the other employees. In other words, he considered it a place to go where he could be actively alone, in order to get away from the regular lunches at his workplace. One person who worked as a physiologist included a visit to the coffee bar in his schedule; he considered a visit to the coffee bar to be a necessity. Typically consultants, and people in more creative professions, use coffee bars as a remedy for getting through a tightly scheduled day.

However, most customers who use coffee bars are much less instrumental in their approach, but even they also identify the importance of being alone as a prerequisite for visiting coffee bars in general. I would term this group of customers those "seeking silent company"; that is to say, they are attracted to the coffee bars because it enables them to feel at home in a space where they know no one. Although they may appreciate a welcoming nod from the baristas, they do not make friends with any of the other clientele, but still find the public space friendly and open.

One of the informants reported that the coffee bar had a compensatory effect in a very specific life situation. She had been going through a divorce, and in this period she had often felt a sense of being lost, especially every second week when she was without her children. She was then often hit by a feeling of complete and destructive loneliness. The quietness and lack of life, especially during the mornings, was painful. But when she adopted a new morning ritual – the visit to the coffee bar next door—her life then became more bearable. Of course, her longings, and her feelings of loss, were not replaced by the coffee bar, but the effect the visits had on her was productive. She slowly started to view her situation in a more optimistic light, and often she could come to feel connected to people, not through conversations, but by sharing the same space, and by the noise and appearance of others.

More than a few of the informants describe their own use of their coffee bar in similar terms; for them it was a place where they could blend in as "an anonymous person," and be respected for the status of being in their own company. Several informants used the expression "reflection" about the type of activity they did in the coffee bar. Many of them considered the combination of a (rather) crowded room with a solitary position as "urbanity": "This is what urbanity means to me, to be alone in a room with other people in the same situation. Sharing something, sharing the coffee, and the notion of sharing it... something like that," said one of the informants, summing up what many of the regular users of these coffee bars seem to experience.

The practice of looking out into the streets, letting their eyes absorb the passing traffic; and also "being looked at"—being part of the window-shopping environment, as it were—was appreciated and described in positive terms by many of the informants. One of them expressed some of these sentiments in the following statement: "You are a part of it, of the town. I look at them and they look at me. That's ok. Some people prefer the countryside, but this here suits me better. I reflect upon life, on the big questions, but also on the small questions when I sit here."

Fourth: How Do They Use the Coffee Bars?

The interviews are important sources for understanding why people use coffee bars, but all of them display the same striking absence of a discussion of the internal design of the coffee bar. This only underscores the crucial importance of observation, because when observing a coffee bar, and how it works, it is possible to register perhaps the only distinct feature it embodies, that makes it so successful as a typology, namely its internal design. To put it briefly: a coffee bar has a design that makes it comfortable for customers to use when they are on their own. When you enter a coffee bar you can easily use the main counter or the window counter. These counters make it possible for an individual to sit down next to another individual without having to establish eye contact. This is similar to the situation in a train or at the theatre. In the case of the coffee bar and the train, one's view can rest on the street or the outside scenery rather than on other individuals within the same space. This enables people to share a rather limited space with one another without being confronted with the other's gaze.

A round table, or a square table, is not among the prescribed ingredients in coffee bar design. They might occur, but as mentioned above, such tables are not a feature that defines a coffee bar. A round table characteristically is a table for two, and two that know each other well, or at least intend to get know each other at a certain level. Only people who are in a familiar situation with each other use the same table. There may not be a "law" forbidding strangers to occupy opposite sides of a round table, but as a social practice it is nonexistent. Therefore cafés and restaurants have a different social character than coffee bars. In this sense, coffee bars are

Figure 9.2   The coffee bar, *Java*. Illustration: Kyrre Holmeseth.

Figure 9.3 The coffee bar, *Evita*. Illustration: Kyrre Holmeseth.

less private, and more public. Figure 9.2 draws attention to how intrinsic this feature is for a coffee bar.

The main counter and window counters function there as the most important design aspect of coffee bars, and the single most important factor explaining their success. These reflections are also visible in the illustrations supporting this chapter. The internal design of a coffee bar—at least the coffee bars shown here—is characterized as providing spaces for individuals, not groups, as seen in Figure 9.3. The individuals I have met and interviewed—even if they use the coffee bars differently—all use them in solitude. Not always, not every time they come to a coffee bar, but in most cases.

Fifth: Solitude Is a State of Being

Both in general terms and in the field of psychology, it is normal to distinguish between solitude and loneliness. While loneliness describes the situation where an individual is involuntarily alone, solitude is often used as a term to define the opposite: a situation where the individual has freely chosen to be alone.

Many informants identified spending time alone in a coffee bar as a meaningful activity. Several underscored the importance of solitude as a tool for "recharging their batteries" and as a helpful pause in a stressful workday where the coffee bar is used instrumentally to achieve reflection and distance. Others, and this constituted the majority of my informants, were less instrumental in their approach, but communicated in different ways that the coffee bar addressed their need for a place where they could contemplate and relax. The subject literature in the field of psychology also identifies these requirements as being characteristic of solitude.[1] This group, the so-called "seeking silent company" group, use the coffee bar as an institution where they can be among others, without being in a state of committed relations. They are there on their own, and voluntarily. Even if they were lonely before they entered the coffee bar, they transform this situation into solitude. The coffee bar—at least those I have studied—seems to embed a social contract of silent community. The majority here are represented by individuals who purposefully choose to be there; and a coffee bar might also be said to produce social capital and an improved state of mental well-being by offering solitude. Even if coffee is the main product in the commercial process in a coffee bar, solitude might be the most interesting social and cultural outcome of these types of institutions.

Note

1. For a more detailed description of solitude, see Long, Christopher R. and Averill, James R. "Solitude: An Exploration of the Benefits of Being Alone;" Journal for the Theory of Social Behaviour 33:1 (2003).

References

Audunson, R. A et al. (2007). Public libraries, social capital, and low intensive meeting places. *Information research*, 12, 4.
Hejer, M. and Reijndorp, A. (2002) *In Search of New Public Domain*. Rotterdam: NAi Publishers.
Holm, E. D. (2010) Coffee and the City: Towards a Soft Urbanity. Volume 45. Con-text. PhD Thesis. Oslo: Oslo School of Architecture and Design.

Long, C. R. and Averill, J. R. (2003) Solitude: an exploration of the benefits of being alone. *Journal for the Theory of Social Behaviour*, 33, 1. Online edition. 30 September 2011.

Jacobs, J. (1961) *The Death and Life of Great American Cities*. New York: Random House.

Oldenburg, R. (1989) *The Great Good Place: Cafes, Coffee Shops, Community Centers, Beauty Parlors, General Stores, Bars, Hangouts, and How They Get You Through the Day*. New York: Paragon House.

Putnam, R. D. (2000) *Bowling Alone: The Collapse and Revival of American Community*. New York: Simon & Schuster.

10

THE CITY, THE CAFÉ, AND THE PUBLIC REALM IN AUSTRALIA

Peter Walters and Alex Broom

More than one billion cups of coffee are consumed in cafés, restaurants, and other outlets each year in Australia, with an increase of 65 percent over the last 10 years.[1] While Australia is still lagging behind nations such as Italy and Japan in terms of drinking coffee outside the home (Ryan, 2006), "Australian coffee culture" has now evolved to the point where it has achieved an important semiotic status. The swirling crema of an espresso coffee is regularly used in marketing campaigns to signify intimacy, warmth, sophistication, and "time out" when advertising products as diverse as apartment developments, holidays, banks, and household-cleaning products. Baristas have become cultural icons and the best are regularly sought out, judged and graded in the same manner as celebrated chefs (e.g., Swan, 2012). Bespoke coffee outlets now sell coffee beans in a manner previously reserved for fine wine, giving consumers a choice of region, variety, and *terroir*, often with the comfort of an ethical provenance in the case of "fair trade" and organic beans. The US coffee behemoth, Starbucks, which has often set the agenda for the development and aesthetics of the contemporary North American coffeehouse (Tucker, 2011), has failed to gain a foothold in the Australian market. This is because small independent coffee shops already had a well-established position offering the "intimacy, personalization, and familiarity of a suburban boutique café" (Patterson, Scott, and Uncles,

2010: 43). Café culture has thus become firmly entrenched in urban Australia, reflecting shifting (and at times polarized) cultural preferences and practices around space, community, and the urban form. Further, as we argue in this chapter, this Australian "café culture" articulates important shifts in class and gender politics, encapsulating forms of social marginality ("inner" vis-à-vis "peripheral"), as well as potentially fostering new forms of community making and resilience. Here we reflect on how these new spaces of sociability are altering the landscape of Australian culture.

The Café, Third Places and Public Realm

What is sociologically interesting about cafés is not that they serve coffee, although the attraction of a mildly addictive substance underwrites the phenomenon (Holtzman, 1990). Rather, it is that cafés have potential to be what Oldenburg (1999) terms "third places," or those places beyond work and home where people can gather and be in the company of others. They are places that provide a link between the public and the private or domestic realms (Lofland, 1998) or, in other words, between work and home. The café tradition, stretching back to its early roots in Europe, is one that encourages unstructured association and low barriers to entry and exit. Cafés are used for people to socialize with friends and colleagues, in a socially comfortable environment or, importantly, to be alone in the company of others. The availability of easily accessible third places plays a vital role in the maintenance of general norms of sociability and civil behavior in circumstances where life has become increasingly segregated and privatized.

There are two arguments for the social benefits of third places such as the café. The first is the "civil society" or cosmopolitan argument where the café can, but not necessarily does, play an important role in the maintenance of both a spatial and a symbolic public realm (Lofland, 1998). The public realm in its abstract sense refers to a cognitive or discursive space that is liberated for the discussion and debate of issues that affect us all, beyond the narrow interests of self and community. The public realm in its spatial sense can be understood as the availability and opportunity for strangers to encounter each other in an "accidental" way. The ability to encounter, if not engage, the stranger (Simmel, 1964), particularly those outside of one's own parochial realm (Lofland, 1998), provides a means of education about "the other," and it would be hoped, an ability to at least deal with, if not embrace, diversity. The public realm and coexistence with strangers are ideas unique to the city. However, in the steadily more privatized world of home, private automobile and place of work or education, these opportunities become increasingly rare. Many Australians live in networked realms that limit their social exposure to only their "own kind." There are few geographical places left in Australia that are so culturally or ethnically homogenous that the opportunity to spend time in a third place would yield no insight into the condition of "the other." Access to the public realm needs to be as wide and easy as possible to enable a properly functioning civil society, comprising "voluntary associations outside the sphere of the state and the economy" (Flyvbjerg, 1998: 210). Iris Marion Young (Young, 1990) describes this type of association as the "an openness to unassimilated otherness" (1990: 318), a vital feature of the "unoppressive city" (1990: 318), and the only way in which cities can avoid the more communally rooted afflictions such as racism, sexism, homophobia, and other intolerance or ridicule of difference.

In contrast to Young's cosmopolitan view of the city is the second argument for the third place, the communitarian one, where places such as cafés have an important role to play in the generation of community, usually conceptualized as community of geographical place.

> Community is an appealing alternative to public life. It promises to provide the pleasures of sociability without the discomforts of the unfamiliar. (Kohn, 2004:193)

In the communitarian worldview, we belong a priori to a community, or at least we should, and the reasons we might not are that processes of individualization and privatization associated with late modernity (Giddens, 1991; Heelas, Lash, and Morris, 1996) have robbed us of the opportunity. Communities in this sense are based on a shared subjectivity (Young, 1990) where we learn how to be responsible and integrated members of that community, it is how children are socialized into behaving in the correct way and it is where associational life is fostered (Frazer, 2000). The communitarian discourse has been strong from policy makers who speak of "strong local communities," "care in the community," and "community capacity building" (Walters and Rosenblatt, 2008). It is communitarianism that underwrites policies such as the Third Way and, more recently, the Big Society in Britain where an increasing burden for public welfare is placed on the shoulders of local communities and the community sector rather than the state. In Australia, there have been a range of communitarian themes culminating most recently in the push for "community resilience" (Australian Government, 2012), the idea that communities need to be sufficiently cohesive and internally well resourced to withstand, and recover from, hardship such as the floods, bush fires and cyclones, and "violent ideologies" (Australian Government, 2012) that have affected various parts of Australia in recent years. In order for communities to develop the shared identity and subsequent social capital required for this level of resilience and internal cohesion, members must have the means by which to grow familiar with each other and to then to grow and cultivate relationships of trust and reciprocity (Putnam, 2000). While cafés alone will not achieve this, they are one form of third place that provides an accessible means of community self-identity without the barriers to entry that are characteristic of other community institutions such as sporting clubs and drinking establishments. The spatial logic of Australian suburbia, where much of the Australian population lives, makes the proliferation of places like cafés problematic, however, before we address this, we turn to some history of cafés and the third place in Australia.

The Third Place in Australia

Australia's history of the third place has been shaped by a combination of the spatial logic of cities, the nature of Australia's evolving immigration policies and by the politics of gender and the family. It is only in the last decade that Australians have begun to emerge from their homes, pubs, and workplaces to drink coffee in the company of others, in cafés. Until World War II, Australians, in the tradition of their British forebears, were tea and beer drinkers (Symons, 2007). The most prevalent form of regular gathering place, or third place, in Australia was the hotel or "pub" where Australian men, particularly working class men, would typically gather after work and on the weekends to socialize. Pubs were mostly located in neighborhoods that now constitute the inner and middle rings of Australian cities, where working class people lived in close proximity to the industries that employed them (Kelly, 1994). Without cars, life was lived for the most part locally. Strong gender roles dictated that men and women worked and socialized separately. The public house or pub, a model imported from Britain, but given its own form in Australia, became the locus for male sociability with strong norms of behavior based on the sustained consumption of beer and the ability "hold your grog." The gendering of pub culture meant that by strong convention, women, except barmaids, were not permitted to enter the public bar (Kelly, 1994; Kirkby, 2003). The pub was such a strong site of masculinity that in 1964, cultural critic Donald Horne wrote that "Men stand around bars asserting their masculinity with such intensity that you half expect them to unzip their flies" (Horne, 1964: 36). Women were permitted to visit the "lounge bar" or "ladies lounge," but it was not the habitual meeting place of women, whose lives were largely confined to work and the domestic realm. It was not until the 1970s that agitation by pioneering feminists saw gender segregation in pubs lifted through anti-discrimination legislation (Kirkby, 2003).

However, by the 1970s pub culture was in decline in Australia. As the population grew, particularly in the second half of the twentieth century, massive tracts of suburbia were developed in capital cities to the point where over 75 percent of Australians now live in suburbs. Postwar suburbs were designed for the automobile and zoned as residential-only tracts, with services, mass retail, and entertainment amenities centrally located around large shopping malls. The inability to work, socialize, and live in the same general area combined with increasingly stringent drink-driving laws marked the demise of the pub as a habitual third place for most (male) Australians. Inner city pubs were renovated and made fashionable according to the needs of inner city gentrifiers beginning in the 1980s, and the demise of the pub as a third place was almost complete. While pubs and clubs still exist, the majority of alcohol in Australia is now consumed in the privacy of the home.

Migration and the Emergence of "Australian" Coffee Culture

While this suburban transformation was taking place, Australia's almost complete demographic dominance by Anglo-Irish migrants began to dilute with the relaxation of Australia's racist White Australia policy in the postwar years. An influx of Southern European migrants to Australia brought with them a love of coffee, and the social rituals that accompany it. The first espresso machines were imported by Italian migrants to inner city Melbourne in the early 1950s (Frost et al., 2010), and it is that tradition that has underwritten the slow development of an Australian coffee, and café, culture in the subsequent 60 years. Café culture in Australia has its roots in those inner city neighborhoods where poor European migrants could afford to first settle, such as Carlton in Melbourne, Surry Hills, and Leichardt in Sydney and New Farm in Brisbane. These migrants from postwar Europe began to replace working class Anglo-Celtic families, who were moving to the new automobile-based suburbs developed in the postwar building boom. The cafés and restaurants established by these migrants provided much of the ethnic character of these inner neighborhoods and which would eventually provide one of the attractions for affluent professional gentrifiers who began to buy and renovate character properties in inner city neighborhoods as land values increased in 1970s and 1980s (Luckins, 2009). The Southern European coffee culture was quickly adopted by these *arrivistes*, who established their own café culture; taking it from its working class roots to something more fashionable and self-conscious.

Politics and Culture Wars

Affluent gentrifiers in Australia have followed a pattern similar to that found in large cities in other Western countries where they have been categorized sociologically by Florida as the "creative classes" (2002) and by Inglehart and others as "postmaterialists"; a well-educated, often professional, demographic who give priority to belonging and self-expression over the materialist priorities of economic and physical security (Inglehart, 2000). This is not to say that postmaterialists are not affluent; traditional class and cultural boundaries are no longer the predictors of affluence in Australia (Suncorp Bank, 2012), but they are more likely to express themselves in terms of cultural pursuits, educational qualifications, and environmental concerns. This distinction in value sets from the "materialist" majority has provided the basis for the "culture wars" in Australia (and elsewhere), as political and media pundits, particularly on the political right, (simplistically) divided the country into "hard working Australian families" who live in the suburbs, and "inner city latte-sipping elites," the latter responsible for various sins such as their irresponsible inner city environmentalism and minority rights agenda. For many of those invested in the culture wars, the inner city love of café culture has become a convenient symbol for mockery of the slaves to fashion of the affluent left and their utopian vision of a Europeanized existence.

> Something has to be done. One of the things I've learned over my years on radio is to put my faith in the commonsense of the Australian rank-and-file. Not in the latte sipping inner-city elites. And not in the political apparatchiks who

work for the factions behind the scenes. (Alan Jones, prominent radio talkback host, CANdo, 2012)

It is certainly the case that the inner city in Australia plays host to the most conspicuously, or self-consciously, "hip" café scene. To take the authors' home city of Brisbane as an example, the neighborhood of West End, with an eclectic and diverse population of just over 8000 people (ABS, 2012), supports 29 different cafés (Urbanspoon, 2012) (this does not include those establishments classified as restaurants). All but one of these cafés is independent. This sort of concentration is repeated across gentrified inner city neighborhoods in other cities in Australia (Urbanspoon, 2012). These cafés are often places where, in addition to playing an important role as third places, patrons are also involved in a particular aesthetic pastime, or performance, rewriting scripts on gender, fashion, and leisure, which are discussed in further detail below.

Depending on the degree of gentrification in these neighborhoods, cafés can be hosts to something approaching a public realm (Lofland, 1998), where a range of people are accommodated and feel comfortable, including the affluent, the poor, the mainstream, the alternative, gay and straight, white, black, Asian, and indigenous. It is still very possible in Brisbane's West End to sit on the sidewalk at a café table and, depending on the time of day, watch a passing parade featuring an array of humanity including the destitute and homeless, the stylishly affluent, the deranged, the intoxicated and the bohemian, older people, children and people from a wide range of ethnicities. The ability to normalize these people as part of the everyday fabric of a vital public realm provides the retail strips of West End and similar neighborhoods a setting for the development of tolerance that allows these people to continue to exist in these areas. The café in a place such as West End, besides playing an important role as a third place, is also important as a "symbolic resource" for a particular lifestyle (Chaney, 1990: 51) accommodated by the fashionable and individualized cafés that occupy inner city neighborhoods.

It is this symbolic capital that eventually leads to its own undoing. As gentrification intensifies, rising property values and the needs and tastes of the affluent eventually marginalize those without the economic or cultural capital to compete in this environment and the neighborhood gradually becomes parochialized by a new dominant culture. However, despite the inevitable parochialism, the inner city is still better able to host a diverse array of Third Spaces as a legacy of its geography and history. The grid pattern of streets, the density of housing, and a preautomobile legacy of retail strips within easy walking distance of homes and workplaces means that people who live in these areas have a natural advantage over those who, through preference or necessity, live in the suburbs. The fact that this amenity exists and the usually vibrant street life that results in turn attracts visitors from outside these areas, eager to experience the atmosphere of cafés, independent retailers and the variety of humanity on offer, further adding to the "buzz" of these inner locations.

Café Culture in Suburbia

Despite its disparagement by the media and political punditry, the desire to drink espresso coffee in cafés Australia has expanded from the inner city "latte set" to the suburbs (AFN, 2012). Spending time in cafés has become a national phenomenon, albeit with different manifestations across geographical and cultural boundaries. The problem with maintaining a viable public realm in Australia has much to do with its urban, and particularly its suburban, character. Australia has been termed a country that was "born modern" (Pusey, 2003: 113), in that its development occurred after the industrial revolution had commenced in Europe. Early migration to Australia was thus based on the expectation of escaping the poverty, squalor and density of a Europe caught between rural and newly industrialized poverty. The emerging middle class in Britain were showing the working classes that a suburban lifestyle of space and safety was a worthwhile aspiration for those with the initiative to emigrate (Davison, 1995). The colonial administration was sensitized to these ambitions and there was no reason or motive to recreate the inner city squalor that characterized the old world (Davison, 1995). So in later years, when Australian cities began to grow rapidly, there was little of the "flight from the inner city" (Chaney, 1990: 55) that occurred in the United States. The suburban ideal had taken hold more or less from the beginning, and the appeal was strong from early white settlement onwards. Strong housing demand and the availability of abundant cheap land provided ideal conditions for the rapid expansion of massive residential-only suburban tracts, characterized by dependence on the automobile and the centralization of retail and other services into large suburban shopping mall complexes (Voyce, 2006). While inner-ring suburbs had a useful mix of retail, residential, and other uses as described above, over time and the with the outward spread of suburbia, even local corner grocery stores disappeared from the suburban landscape and any possibility for local communal focal points such as cafés were lost as development took place according to the logic of automobile travel and the economies of scale of mass retail. This style of suburban residential development has shown little change, although the pace of development on the edges of Australian cities has slowed as land has become scarcer and authorities have recognized the environmental and infrastructure costs of this type of development. However, it has left much of the Australian population few options for a local form of third place in their residential environments.

The suburb in Australia was for much of its history an expression of individual autonomy, rather than of a collectivity. As Pusey has observed,

> Australians take a distinctively cool and modern view of community...Australia was born modern, it never had the deep soil layer of pre-modern "primordial," religiously infused, village and rural community that is such a feature of older societies – including the United States – that were formed before the Industrial Revolution. We do not have the same motherhood feelings about communities and communitarian "habits of the heart" as Americans do. (Pusey, 2003: 113)

The communitarianism that has dominated discourse in recent years has, in effect, been retrofitted to the strong individualism that marked the Australian suburban landscape through most of the twentieth century. This individualism, it could be argued, has been spatially determined and for many has meant isolation. This is particularly so for women, many of whom felt the isolation of suburbia (Bryson and Thompson, 1972; Egar and Sarkissian, 1985).

For the most part, residents of outer suburbs are required to travel by car to visit cafés. For those who do, shopping malls and suburban shopping strips, are where busy cafés are located. It can be difficult to see what sort of comparison might be made with those of the bohemian and studied cool of the inner city. Shopping mall cafés are becoming increasingly corporate, the suburbs are the home of national franchises such as Coffee Club, Zafarellos and Gloria Jeans, Australia's home grown versions of Starbucks. It is these organizations that have the economic critical mass to negotiate rental agreements with the corporations that operate Australia's shopping malls. The coffee on offer moves further away from the purist espresso experience, with choices like jumbo skinny lattes and hazelnut cappuccinos becoming more commonplace.

The shopping mall café serves a dual purpose—beyond its self-evident function of providing a place where shoppers can sit down, eat, and drink, it also provides a focus for the appearance of activity that is less obviously the performance of pure consumption than the rest of the mall. The mall café can be incorporated into the narrative myth that the mall somehow acts as a community hub, that it is as natural as a neighborhood (Dovey, 2008). As Chaney observes, the only other areas where shoppers can rest in a mall are benches and other types of seating area:

> They are meant to be places where the weary can rest and the informal networks of community life be reaffirmed. They are indeed often crowded but with much of the vitality of station waiting rooms. (Chaney, 1990: 59).

The shopping mall can be thought of as what Augé (1995) refers to as a "non-place" or a place that does not hold the imagination of people; these are transitory spaces in where it is difficult to make lasting social relationships, which are designed and used primarily for an instrumental purpose, in this case retail consumption. Other examples are the airport terminal, or the highway service station. Non-places give few clues to where they are located in time and space, their physical form taking on a generic "place-less" quality. These places are social, but not communal (Dovey, 2008: 139). The ability to sustain successful third places in this type of environment is constrained by the nature of the non-place because, according to Auge, "place is good because we meet people and we establish relationships there, while the non-place is bad because there everyone is a stranger to everyone else" (Skira, 2009: 126). While Auge is perhaps a little stark in his binary description, his point is a valid one, in that people invest little of themselves in a non-place and it accounts for little of their identity. It is difficult then to invest much meaning into a café experience, at least in terms of its potential as a third *place* in an environment so single-mindedly constructed both physically and symbolically for retail consumption.

We should balance this view somewhat with the observation that the Australian retail sector has yet to be completely transformed by the WalMart-led "big box" phenomenon as it has in North America (Parlette and Cowen, 2011) and Australian shopping malls are now being physically transformed and symbolically repositioned away from the massive disorienting complexes, all under one roof, that characterized the first generation of shopping malls. These newer shopping centres are less intimidating in their scale, have a combination of indoor and outdoor retail, eating and drinking options and allow the penetration of natural light. The fact there does exist the foundations of a national café culture has meant that developers are now able to incorporate features of this cultural artefact into newer retail spaces, although purists would argue that the suburban mall café could only ever be a facsimile of the authentic café. The fact remains that shopping malls remain for many, particularly the old and the young, as relatively regulated havens from the "unpredictability" of the outside environment (Tyndall, 2010). Although this is in contradiction to idea of a true public realm, which encourages the citizen to become comfortable with the unfamiliar, in the absence of a more utopian vision for the suburbs, people as active agents are able to reinterpret and resist (de Certeau, 1984) the dominant uses of spaces (Tyndall, 2010). It would be both arrogant and simplistic to imagine that in these environments cafés could not play host to at least a parochial, if not a fully public realm (Lofland, 1998).

Gender and Third Places: The War on Alternative Masculinities in Australia

Before we conclude, it is also important to include a further discussion of the gender implications of the contrast we have illustrated between the third places as manifest in the cafés of inner city Australia and the quite different gender expectations of the "mainstream" of Australia more common to the suburbs. In terms of gender, the shopping mall café has turned the idea of a third place on its head if compared to the situation that existed when Australian still had a thriving pub culture. The shopping mall in its regulated daytime manifestation is still largely the realm of women, and stereotypically reluctant males. While males are no less consumption-oriented than women in Australian society, their consumptive spaces lie outside the shopping mall, which are dominated by clothing, household goods, supermarkets, and departments stores. If the Australian pub posed strong customary barriers to participation by women then the Australian shopping mall café provides a less robust, but still symbolically significant barrier to the working male in Australian culture.

On the other hand, the emergence of inner city third places, such as West End in Brisbane or Surry Hills in Sydney, has brought with it a series of important gender and class-related changes. The notion of the urban "metrosexual" male, for example, is often tied within popular culture to the presence of inner city cafés (and gentrified pubs) and a more "feminized" lifestyle, placing importance on a self-conscious attention to a purist coffee experience, fashion, and male grooming. In order to understand such dynamics, some discussion of normative gender constructs within Australian popular culture and the interplay with class is important. Connell wrote the classic text *Masculinities* in 1995, which provided an important understanding of heteronormative masculinities within Australian culture, including the marginalization of other expressions of gender and nonhetero sexualities. Different forms of third place provide another way into examining the socio-spatial expressions of gender, and in this case masculinities, with various components of what Connell called hegemonic masculinity, perhaps challenged by these very places. Or perhaps more accurately, the diversification and polarization of masculinities in the context of suburban and urban cultural shifts; a process contesting existing normative framings of *what is* Australian masculinity. Specifically, we argue here that the persistence of classic hegemonic features of antipodean masculinity including: physical strength, silence, or "silent types"; toughness and violence; stoicism; and so on, may be increasingly undermined within certain inner city scenes/spaces where other ideas about what is masculine are growing (or have been established). This is not to create an overly binary view of gender expression across city spaces. Indeed, there is crossover, greyness, and fluidity in how gender is done across populations, and city spaces. However, the existence of very clearly discrete inner third places with certain politics and situated within certain ideas about lifestyle and values, inflects gender performances and expression. As Judith Butler (1990) argues, gender is a "repeated stylization of the body, a set of repeated acts within a highly rigid regulatory frame that congeal over time to produce the appearance of substance, of a natural sort of being" (p. 33); gender is "done" or "accomplished" in everyday life (Connell, 1995). Inner city third places are new spaces within which gender is done, and in some respects quite differently as compared to outer, suburban areas. These inner city areas have accommodated "alternative," but still normative, ideas about what men do, or perhaps what men are permitted to do. We can see the ways in which this actually does transgress wider cultural ideas, many of which are also class based, about what *real* men do within popular culture whereby the idea of the latte sipping, inner city metrosexual male does not sit well with the imagined "hard, heterosexual ANZAC."[2] Below is scene from a popular television show by comedian Ronnie Johns who takes on the persona of Australian criminal icon and "hard man" Mark "Chopper" Reid. While meant to be a parody, it has now been viewed now by more than 2.6 million people on YouTube, and is firmly entrenched in Australian popular culture to "out" nonmasculine behavior, the clip captures some of the clash of masculinities within Australian culture:

> *Ronnie Johns*: Hello, how the fuck are ya? Chopper Reid here. One thing I noticed all across Australia is that people are having a winge, having a sook, or cry about it. If the ANZACS were around today I reckon they would be fuckin' spewing. Australia needs to harden the fuck up…
> [Walks up to a young man on a city street]
> *Ronnie Johns*: This is Peter, and he drinks soymilk in his coffee. Oh look at me, I'm lactose intolerant! "Why don't you try a mochachino of harden the fuck up Peter?"
> [Series of other people who are told to "harden the fuck up"]
> *Ronnie Johns*: So, come on Australia. Take your skirt off, cancel your manicure, grow a moustache and harden the fuck up.

The clip captures two important themes, the mythological components of Australian normative masculinities and the sense that this norm is being challenged by gendered values that the inner city (latte drinkers) and various spaces within the Australian city may be now be promoting. On Australian conservative talkback radio and within sport commentary, such narratives around a decline in masculinity and male potency due to the "inner city lifestyle" are heard regularly. That is, the idea that shifting, inner city masculinities are compromising what it is to be an Australian male. What is important in this chapter is how cafés as third spaces contribute to, or are tied to, such dynamics. In some respects, the inner city café has become a space for resistance to hetero-normative masculinities and a space for the production of new expressions of Australian masculinities (whether metrosexual or for protest by Other marginalized expressions of masculinity). It is of course important not to reify such expressions as indeed there is potential for the emergence of new normative "alternative" masculinities within such spaces. Metrosexuality, for example, has many of the marginalizing and normative features of other hegemonic masculine forms. The coffee sipping (male) "minority" of high-income professionals with white collar jobs and others in the creative classes necessarily undermines many features of working class Australian hegemonic masculinities, just by their lack of need for these various traits in their labor and life styles. As such, gender expression is shaped to a place and to everyday practices, and while still carefully distinguished from performances of "femininity," takes on a manifestation of the inner city in fashion, coffee culture and aesthetically based social distinction. Such expressions also become exclusive and normative due to access to those resources that allow people to live in the inner city, and to maintain the required patterns of consumption for this type of identity work.

This inevitably leads to a discussion about class and as shown in Ronnie Johns' clip, war between the "real men" and the latte sipping men of inner city Sydney, Melbourne or Brisbane. While we do not argue for a spatially determined understanding of gender expression in contemporary Australia cities, we do suggest that these third spaces provide a useful window into shifting gender relations, particularly between groups of men across social class and urban spaces, that are unsettling for many in wider Australian culture. What is specifically unsettling is that inner city third spaces are supporting and embracing types of identity work, forms of "manliness" and gender work, that move against the imagined "Australian way." In colloquial terms it is distinctly "un-Australian," a notion utilized rhetorically in Australian popular culture and as a political device to *Other* forms of discourse, practice and belief not considered resonant with core Australian values (in this case, easy going, laid back, "salt of the earth" normative masculinities). Despite the counter-movement again contemporary metrosexualities, we argue that such gender practices are likely to be sustained and prosper given the economic and cultural influence of those living and thriving within these third places and inner urban spaces. As such, while Ronnie might ask us to "harden the fuck up," and indeed, many Australians may want inner city dwellers to do just this, it is perhaps more likely that class conflict and forms of social polarization will persist and even be intensified with the rise of the inner city third place, for the all of the spatial, cultural and gendered reasons we have examined.

Conclusion

We have provided a both a historical, and a geographical tour of coffee culture and the café in Australia. The Australian experience is unique in that its cities are much closer to those of the United States in terms of patterns of urbanization, particularly suburbanization. Australians embraced the modernist project of single use residential zoning, an automobile-based spatial logic and the centralization of massed-retail that now characterize most Australians' residential experience. At the same time Australia has also, due to its postwar migration history, developed a cultural appreciation for coffee, which is much more European than North American in its character.

However, to complete the European imaginary, one needs to travel from the suburbs to the inner city of Australia, where an early industrial spatial logical and the subsequent aesthetic preferences of gentrifiers to preserve the perceived authenticity of an ethnic legacy have meant that the independent coffee shop, the destination in-itself, has thrived. The inner city café is a place to linger, to be the company of the stranger and in its less parochial form can contribute the establishment of the sort of norms of tolerance of difference to which Iris Marion Young (1990) referred. The inner city and the café have also provided space for new expressions of gender. A potentially less "brutal," but also normative, masculinity, and a more inclusive femininity can exist in these places.

However, for the vast majority of Australians who live in the suburbs, the embrace of coffee culture, while no less enthusiastic, finds expression in different ways to the inner city. The centralized shopping mall is a far more abstract place, created by capital and more singular in its purpose (Lefebvre, 1991). It requires a certain degree of resistance to lay claim to a functioning third place, in a shopping mall or strip-mall, in circumstances where "hanging out" is neither facilitated nor encouraged. Unlike the inner city, the shopping mall is also a gendered space, retaining as it does a legacy of gender roles inherited from modernity where women shop and men work.

To return to our two possible purposes for the third place, the cosmopolitan and the communitarian, it would appear that the café in Australia, offers some potential as a cosmopolitan third place, in those neighborhoods where difference and diversity are accepted and celebrated as markers of cultural capital and where historical good fortune has provided the spatial logic that embeds cafés in a locality. However, the potential of the café as a third place, even in its communitarian manifestation, is more difficult in the suburban expanse where most Australians live. In this regard, the Australian suburban dweller has been short-changed by history. Planners and property developers are slowly seeing the benefits of designing new residential spaces that take into account people's natural proclivity to cross paths with their fellow humans through the construction of mixed use and walkable neighborhoods. However, it is the legacy of the modernist project that determined the huge tracts of automobile based suburbia that almost inevitably reinforces much of the cultural and gendered divide that we have discussed in this chapter.

Notes

1. See www.acta.org.au.
2. ANZAC (Australian and New Zealand Army Corps) is the collective name given to Australian and New Zealand soldiers in World War I. Their bravey and stoicism have become an important national myth and, to many, a standard to which masculinity is compared.

References

AFN (2012) Aussie Café Culture Accounts for 'Biggest Growth in Coffee.' http://www.ausfoodnews.com.au/2010/03/04/aussie-cafe-culture-accounts-for-biggest-growth-in-coffee.htm.

ABS (2012) *Census 2011*. Canberra Australian Bureau of Statistics.

Augé, M. (1995) *Non-Places: Introduction to an Anthropology of Supermodernity*. London New York, Verso.

Australian Government (2012) *Resilient Communities*. http://www.resilientcommunities.gov.au, accessed September, 25.

Bryson, L. and Thompson, F. (1972) *An Australian Newtown: Life and Leadership in a Working-Class Suburb*. Harmondsworth: Penguin Books.

Butler, J. (1990) *Gender Trouble: Feminism and the Subversion of Identity*. New York: Routledge.

CANdo (2012) *Alan Jones calls for major constitutional change*. http://www.cando.org.au/updates/86-alan-jones-calls-for-major-constitutional-change, accessed July 9.

Chaney, D. (1990) Subtopia in gateshead: the metrocentre as a cultural form. *Theory, Culture & Society*, 7, 49–68.

Connell, R. W. (1995) *Masculinities*. Sydney: Allen & Unwin.

Davison, G. (1995) Australia: the first suburban nation? *Journal of Urban History*, 22, 40–74.

de Certeau, M. (1984) *The Practice of Everyday Life*. Berkeley, London: University of California Press.

Dovey, K. (2008) *Framing Places: Mediating Power in Built Form*. London, New York: Routledge.

Egar, R. and Sarkissian, W. (1985) Coping with the suburban nightmare: developing community supports in Australia. *Sociological Focus*, 18, 119–125.

Florida, R. L. (2002) *The Rise of the Creative Class: And How It's Transforming Work, Leisure, Community and Everyday Life*. New York, NY: Basic Books.

Flyvbjerg, B. (1998) Habermas and Foucault: thinkers for civil society? *The British Journal of Sociology*, 49, 210–233.

Frazer, E. (2000) Communitarianism. In Webster, F., Browning, G. K., and Halcli, A. (Eds) Understanding Contemporary Society: Theories of the Present. London and, Thousand Oaks, CA: Sage Publications, pp. 178–190.

Frost, W., et al. (2010). Coffee Culture, Heritage and Destination Image: Melbourne and the Italian model. In Jolliffe, L. (Ed.) *Coffee Culture, Destinations and Tourism*. Bristol, UK: Channel View Publications, pp. 99–110.

Giddens, A. (1991) *Modernity and Self Identity: Self and Society in the Late Modern Age*. Cambridge: Polity Press.

Heelas, P., Lash, S., and Morris, P. (1996) *Detraditionalization: Critical Reflections on Authority and Identity*. Cambridge, Mass.: Blackwell.

Holtzman, S. G. (1990) Caffeine as a model drug of abuse. *Trends in Pharmacological Sciences*, 11, 355–356.

Horne, D. (1964) *The Lucky Country: Australia in the Sixties*. Ringwood: Penguin.

Inglehart, R. (2000) Globalization and postmodern values. *The Washington Quarterly*, 23, 215–228.

Kelly, W. J. (1994) *Booze Built Australia*. Brisbane: Queensland Classic Books.

Kirkby, D. (2003) "Beer, glorious beer": Gender politics and Australian popular culture. *Journal of Popular Culture*, 37, 244–256.

Kohn, M. (2004) *Brave New Neighborhoods*. New York, NY: Routledge.

Lefebvre, H. (1991) *The Production of Space*. Oxford: Blackwell.

Lofland, L. H. (1998) *The Public Realm: Exploring the City's Quintessential Social Territory*. Hawthorne, NY: Aldine de Gruyter.

Luckins, T. (2009) Gentrification and cosmopolitan leisure in inner-urban Melbourne, Australia, 1960s–1970s. *Urban Policy and Research*, 27, 265–275.

Oldenburg, R. (1999) *The Great Good Place*. New York: Marlowe.

Parlette, V. and Cowen, D. (2011) Dead malls: suburban activism, local spaces, global logistics. *International Journal of Urban and Regional Research*, 35, 794–811.

Patterson, P.G., Scott, J., and Uncles, M. D. (2010) How the local competition defeated a global brand: the case of Starbucks. *Australasian Marketing Journal*, 18, 41–47.

Pusey, M. (2003) *The Experience of Middle Australia: The Dark Side of Economic Reform*. Cambridge, Port Melbourne: Cambridge University Press.

Putnam, R. D. (2000). *Bowling Alone: The Collapse and Revival of American Community*. New York: Simon & Schuster.

Ryan, R. (2006) Faster coffee. *Hospitality*: online.

Simmel, G. (1964) The Stranger. In Simmel, G. (Ed.) The Sociology of Georg Simmel. New York: Free Press, p. 445.

Skira (2009) *Places and Non-Places – A Conversation with Marc Augé*. http://onthemove.autogrill.com/gen/lieux-non-lieux/news/2009-01-26/places-and-non-places-a-conversation-with-marc-auge, accessed 25 September.

Suncorp Bank (2012) *Wages Report May 2012: "The Emergence of the Fluoro Collar Worker."* Brisbane Suncorp Bank.

Swan, J. (2012) Dish-Washing Barista Rides Orient Espresso to Peak of Recognition. *Sydney Morning Herald*. Sydney: Fairfax.
Symons, M. (2007). *One Continuous Picnic: A Gastronomic History of Australia*. Parkville, Vic.: Melbourne University Publishing.
Tucker, C. M. (2011) *Coffee Culture Local Experiences, Global Connections*. New York: Routledge.
Tyndall, A. (2010) 'It's a public, I reckon': publicness and a suburban shopping mall in Sydney's southwest. *Geographical Research*, 48, 123–136.
Urbanspoon (2012) *Urbanspoon (website)*. http://www.urbanspoon.com, accessed August 10, 2012.
Voyce, M. (2006) Shopping malls in Australia: the end of public space and the rise of 'consumerist citizenship'? *Journal of Sociology*, 42, 269–286.
Walters, P. and Rosenblatt, T. (2008) Co-operation or co-presence? The comforting ideal of community in a master planned estate. *Urban Policy and Research*, 26, 397–413.
Young, I. M. (1990) The Ideal of Community and the Politics of Difference. In Nicholson, L. J. (Ed.) *Feminism/Postmodernism*. New York: Routledge, pp. 300–323.

Index

Australia pub, 189–90
Australian coffee culture, 185
Australian suburbia, 188
Australian values, 200
auto-ethnography, 110–12

belonging, 100
Bergen (Norway), 29
Berlin, 29
Brisbane, Australia, 192–3

Café Central, 43
cafe worker, 93–4
Chicago School of Sociology, 106
city planners, 26
civil society, 186
color judgements, 133–4
communal awareness, 103, 109, 120–2
communal interacting, 112
community life, 25
community resilience, 188
community, 147, 151, 164–8
Copenhagen, 24
cosmopolitanism, **26, 186**
creative class, 191
culture wars (Australia), 191
customer service, 137–9

diary shop, 31, **32, 33**, 34, **35, 36**, 37
diversions, 160
dukani, 49–52

elite, 82–3
English Coffee House, 45, 68–71
espresso machine, 190
ethnomethodology, 128–9, 130

fair trade, 185
familiarity bonds, 2, 82
flaneur, 85
Free Wi-fi, 93

gemeinschaft and gesellschaft, 104–5, 120
gender (in Australia), 189–90, 197–206
gentrification, 27, **36**, 37, 39, 36–7, 191–3
global chains, 40
glocalization, 150, 165–6
grass root democracy, 19–20

HBO, 7
health care, 32
Hollywood, 37
home, 159
household, 25, 30, 31, 39, 40

IKEA, 36
inattention, 159
In between space, 93
individualism, 195
instructions, 129–131
involvement shield, 159
Italian migration to Australia, 190

kitchen table society, 34–5
Kutaisi entertainment, 61–2

late modernity, 188
loners, 94–96

meeting place, 34
metrosexual, 197–9
microhistory, 25
middle class, 26, 27, 30, 36, 39
milk, 23, **32**, **33**, **35**, 38
mothers, 98
mutual aid society, 17

neotribe, 107
networked individualism, 152, 165–6
new social movements, 82

organic beans, 185

parochial realm, 193
people watching, 161
place makers, 93–4, 161–8
post-materialism, 191
private control, 166–8
private realm, 186
privatism, 148–50, 152–2, 164–9
productivity, 157–61
public realm, 186
public solitude, 94, 101

regulars, 91–3
routine, 100

satellite village, 25
serendipity, 163
shopping mall, 195–6
sidewalk cafe, 18–19

skill (barista), 127–9
small shops, **26**, 27, **28**, **35**, 37
social capital, 149
social class, 83–4
social guest, 96–8
social networks, 148–50, 152, 164, 168
social polarization, 201
solidarity, organic/mechanical, 105, 120
solitude, 161
Starbucks, 71–5, 185, 195
subtle ties, 121–2
suburbia, 27, 36, 194

takeaway customer, 90–1
talkback radio, 199
the Great Depression, 30, 31
The usual, 93
third place, 7–20, 24–6, 75, 93, 109, 186, 198
true mobiles, 94, 157–61, 164–7
trust, 115–17

upper, 26, 33
urban architecture, 27
urban life, 25
urbanism, 24, 31, 35
urbanization, 25

Vienna, 29
Viennese Café, 45

Walmart, 196
weak ties, 120–1
White Australia policy, 190
workflow, 140
working class, 26, 32, 34
workplace studies, 107–8
World War II, 27, 32

Printed in the United States of America